LEAD
WITH
GRACE

Jessica Cabeen

LEAD WITH GRACE

Leaning into
the Soft Skills of Leadership

Lead with Grace
© 2019 by Times 10 Publications

These books are available at special discounts when purchased in quantity for premiums, promotions, fundraising, and educational use. For inquiries and details, contact us at WeLeadForward.com.

Published by Times 10
Highland Heights, OH
Times10Books.com

Cover Design by Najdan Mancic
Interior Design by Steven Plummer
Editing by Carrie White-Parrish
Proofreading by Jennifer Jas

Library of Congress Cataloging-in-Publication Data is available.

ISBN: 978-1-948212-16-8
First Printing: August, 2019

Dedication

This book is dedicated to my mentors.

First, to my mentor, Ron. Thank you for showing me how to lead and live with grace in my interactions and actions. I am grateful for everything you have taught me, and that you stuck with me through the valleys and mountains.

And to my husband, Rob. I am so grateful for your belief in me, which is sometimes more than I have in myself. Thank you for joining me on this journey and for always pushing me to live and lead with grace in life, at school, and at home.

Perhaps you were born for such a time as this.
—ESTHER 4:14 (PARAPHRASED)

Acknowledgments

Thank you, Mark Barnes, Carrie White-Parrish, Jennifer Jas, and the Lead Forward team for giving me this opportunity to share this work with others.

Table Of Contents

Editor's Foreword

READING THIS BOOK is like sitting down for a conversation with Jessica Cabeen at a coffee shop. Imagine you are across from her, the clink of mugs and the hiss of steaming milk softening the sounds of voices nearby. Between sips of latte, Jessica tells a story about one of her early epic fails as a middle school principal. You lean in so she doesn't have to broadcast the details, but she is not embarrassed. Her stories are real, she is authentic, and she describes how she gracefully—or not so—handled each situation. When she shares her strategies for doing better next time, you tuck them away, knowing you'll need them yourself. When it's time to go and the last chapter comes to a close, you've caught a vision for what life-changing leadership looks like.

School leader, author, and keynote speaker Jessica Cabeen wrote *Lead with Grace* primarily for leaders in education—teacher leaders, principals, superintendents—yet it also applies to those of us in business, the community, and beyond.

Jessica knows about the soft skills of leadership. She currently serves as a middle school principal, but took a meandering path to get there, learning lessons and picking flowers of grace along the way. She was a music therapist, autism teacher, special education teacher, and assistant middle school principal before becoming principal of an all-kindergarten center. There, she enjoyed sticky peanut butter hugs and steered the school into regional prominence before heading back to middle school as a principal. And she's an award-winning one, gracefully accepting awards for leadership in the early learning setting and being named the Minnesota National Distinguished Principal in 2017.

This is Jessica's third book and her second book for Times 10 Publications (the first was *Hacking Early Learning*, part of the Hack Learning Series).

As a member of the Times 10 editorial team, I help refine the books so the audiences more powerfully connect with the messages the authors share. Part of the beauty of serving as a book editor is the ability to personally soak up value from the books I polish. I was excited to work on the Lead Forward Series and its gold mine of ideas, primarily by women authors, to turn readers into better leaders.

I admit when I first heard the title *Lead with Grace: Leaning Into the Soft Skills of Leadership*, I thought, "I already do a pretty good job with the soft skills." It only took a few pages before I understood how much room I had left to grow. I think back a few years to my corporate communications leadership roles where I was responsible for engaging 15,000 employees in the company mission, serving as an emcee for employee meetings with audiences in the hundreds, and leading a small team—and the vast opportunities to show grace and vulnerability in difficult situations. If Jessica's book had been available, I would've dog-eared the pages. I would've bought twenty copies and passed them out to the leadership team. What a beautiful work environment it would be if more people learned to lead with grace!

Few leaders seem to excel in these skills, but anyone can learn to adopt them. Pressures and demands in a 24/7 world of technology mean more than ever that we need to establish authentic relationships. We need to lead with grace and authenticity.

Stories Strategies Moving Forward

Lead with Grace is the second book in the Lead Forward Series, which shares the journeys of teacher leaders doing amazing work and how others can learn and grow from their examples. The first book was Sanée Bell's *Be Excellent on Purpose*, and the next two are *Quiet Kids Count* by Chrissy Romano Arrabito and *Modern Mentor* by Suzy Brooks and Matthew Joseph.

Within these pages, Jessica shares forty-five stories as humble examples of epic fails and beautiful experiences that all helped her learn to lead forward. Readers will nod in understanding and laugh in relatability as she reveals the grace required to not only get through the worst days but to thrive within a bigger mission. Each chapter includes Stories followed by Strategies with specific, actionable, and practical steps to apply these principles to your environment, before wrapping up with a Moving Forward section and a compelling charge.

Lead Forward Journal

You'll find a Lead Forward Journal at the end of each chapter as a spot for you to write your thoughts and reflect on how to apply the insights to your life and work. We invite you to share your journal entries (not the personal ones, of course) online at #LeadForward. The journals also serve as study guides and supplemental tools for book study groups.

As you will discover, leaning into the soft skills of leadership does not mean being a soft leader. If you want to work at a school where every staff member thinks you're just the nicest person ever, this is not the book for you. If you want somebody to tell you how to lead, look elsewhere. But if you're ready to learn from your experiences and those of others, to engage your team in the discussion, and to Lead Forward—read on! Sip that last splash of latte while it's still warm, then get out there and lead with grace and authenticity. Your students and stakeholders are counting on you.

— Jennifer Jas, Chief Editor at WordswithJas.com and Member of the Times 10 Publications Editorial Team

Homing In and Owning the Soft Skills of Leadership

RACE. WHAT DOES it really mean? When you look it up in the Merriam-Webster dictionary, it is defined as many things: a virtue, a favor given to others, a privilege, a character trait, and even a prayer. For me, as a leader at work and at home, grace touches all aspects of life and impacts how I live, communicate, and serve others.

I believe that leading with grace means you are willing to learn something every day, and forgive yourself for mistakes along the way.

Now more than ever, we need grace. With technology, we interact with families, students, and staff on a 24/7 basis, rather than just during the school day or working hours. Pressures and demands can change us into a person who favors "likes" and stops looking for authentic interactions. But we need those interactions to establish deep relationships with those we live with and lead. Back in the day, the most competition and self-consciousness I experienced was when the laminator put a wrinkle in the artifacts I was putting up on my bulletin board. Today's educators must compete with Teachers Pay Teachers, Twitter, Pinterest, Facebook Groups,

YouTube channels, and being tagged on articles and ideas from friends and coworkers. These things can all tip the scales on their stress levels, and leave them feeling as if their performance can never be enough.

And the polarization of social media is harder than anything I experienced as a young teacher without the internet. I cringe when I see someone create a post they put their heart into, only to see others tag, tweet, and comment about the flaws in the post. And parents are not always helping. Teachers pull into parking lots every morning hoping to get through the day without an accusatory email or a shaming post from one parent or another. Honestly, I struggle with setting expectations for students on their use of social media when I know many of them have adult models who directly contradict every social media grace we want to set. With this pulse and pace, we as teachers need to stop and practice grace—both with ourselves and with others—just to keep moving forward.

Lead with Grace will give you the starting point. Grace provides you with an opportunity to be better than you were before, but only if you know how to use it. Grace starts with communication—with others and with ourselves. In a time when people would rather text than talk, we face the challenge of bringing back kindness, compassion, and caring in our conversations. When a tweet can be screenshotted and sent to everyone, it is essential that every word we say has intention and meaning, in any context.

Leading with grace also requires a sharp focus on soft skills. Now, these skills are not easily taught from a textbook. Instead, they are modeled and applied through trial, error, and reflection. You'll find that much of this book incorporates stories about attempts, failures, and the learnings that came from them—and how those learnings can grow and expand into grace. Throughout the book, these soft skills manifest themselves in the following ways:

- Grace of Authenticity
  - Confidence
  - Intention
  - Assertiveness
  - Passion
- Grace of Vulnerability
  - Honesty
  - Care
  - Risk-taking
  - Learning from mistakes
  - Problem-solving
- Grace of Empathy
  - Listening
  - Practicing patience
  - Gratefulness
  - Openness
- Grace of Integrity
  - Maintaining a strong work ethic
  - Managing time and tasks
  - Focus
  - Confidence

Utilizing these soft skills allows us to build deeper relationships, increase clarity in our conversations, set firm boundaries, and maintain positive attitudes and outlooks in our lives—and in the lives of the students we're leading. We find ourselves in a world where common courtesies and graces are slipping. *Lead with Grace* will give you the tools to put grace back into the busy pace of today's society.

How will you know if this is the right book for you? Perhaps you are:

- Ready to prioritize soft skills while leading in work and life.

- Recognizing that this is the time to stand up and address conflict in your classroom, workplace, or a social situation in a productive way.

- Frustrated with the negative talking, texting, tweeting, and tagging that is occurring in real life and online, and ready to be the change.

- Exhausted from constantly being on, engaged, and busy, which causes you guilt or shame when you want to rest.

Perhaps this is the time to commit to leading with an intentional use of soft skills in your interactions. Maybe you are ready to listen to others with an open mind and an empathetic ear. Now might be the time to learn from your mistakes by sharing your fears with those close to you. This could be the moment you decide to lead and live by sharing gratitude with others instead of holding grudges.

If so, this is the time to give yourself the grace to be who you have always wanted to be.

It won't necessarily be easy. It's going to take work to get to know yourself even better. Grace is messy, it is imperfect, and it is always a work in progress. But through these stories of missteps and learnings, I hope you can walk away with essential practices and exercises that allow you to feel more confident in yourself and how you extend grace to others in your day-to-day activities, and in complicated situations.

Today is the right time to incorporate grace in leadership. There's no better time to start building and enhancing our soft skills to elevate interactions and relationships. Together, we can establish breathing space for you, and put a pause on the busywork, replacing it with reflection, forgiveness, and gratitude. Using those soft skills, I'll provide you with ways to lead at your best, even in the worst of circumstances.

Thank you for joining me on this journey! I look forward to learning your story and finding ways to work with you to strengthen our callings and support each other in the work we are blessed to do. Join the conversation at #LeadForward and #LeadwithGrace to share your experiences, ask questions, and brainstorm new ideas!

Dream big, live colorfully, lead boldly, and elevate every action and interaction with a touch of grace.

Authentic Grace

Be Unapologetic in Your Leadership Style

*There are only twenty-four hours in a day; we need to
quit trying to be awesome, and instead be wise.*
— JEN HATMAKER, *FOR THE LOVE*

The Frogger Career

DO YOU REMEMBER the video game *Frogger*? The object of
the game was to get your frogs safely across the river and
road. You had to dodge the vehicles on the road and then
use logs to get across the river. Growing up, I loved that game and
the creative logic behind it. Sometimes, to get ahead, you had to
take a step back or sideways.

Too often, we get caught up in other people's perceptions, so
much so that we stop moving altogether. Instead of thinking about
your moves in terms of perfection, focus on the process. You are
uniquely you, and the road you travel should mirror *you*, not the
life you think others want you to lead.

If you look at my résumé, you will see I have taken the path less
traveled to get to where I am today. The degrees I achieved certainly

haven't matched other people's expectations! In college, while my friends were taking their education classes, I was taking psychology and biology classes, along with my music courses. When they were working in schools, I was in nursing homes, hospitals, and prison settings. When they went into their student teaching, I left for Dixon, Illinois, and spent nine months working in a residential and day treatment school for teenagers. When people share stories from their first year of teaching, I talk about how I was helping an adult with visual and cognitive impairments become more comfortable navigating his group home, or the client who suffered a traumatic brain injury from a motorcycle accident, and how lyric analysis was helping him move forward from the anger of his life being dramatically changed. When I talked with new educators and helped them get started, I learned I needed an elevator speech to explain why I'd taken the path I'd taken, rather than one that matched my friends' paths.

That elevator speech starts with a specific *Frogger* log coming into view. The Saint Paul Public Schools association was seeking non-traditional students for a grant that provided alternative paths into a traditional teaching license. I applied and was accepted in the collaborative urban educator program, and for the next two years, I was a music therapist in Saint Paul schools by day and a college student by night, getting my teaching license in special education. After the program, I taught in autism classrooms for three years. I was then invited to join the special education administrative team at the district office of the Saint Paul Public Schools as an intern while finishing my coursework as a special education director. I was on track for a full-time position in this department when a new obstacle jumped in front of me.

Suddenly, I was a few logs to the left in rural southeastern Minnesota, in a district significantly smaller than what I was used to.

But I didn't let it get me down. After a decade in various positions, I landed the one I thought I was called to lead: the assistant principal at a middle school. I loved the day-to-day interactions with students and the opportunity to build relationships with them. Three years into that position, though, the logs in the leadership journey once again stopped moving to my advantage. I had an option to take a jump sideways (or backward) and took a position at a kindergarten center. Many of my colleagues thought I was taking a lesser position, moving down the ladder instead of up. I didn't have much practical experience for the position, and I was going to have to work extremely hard to catch up to the people I was working with. Some thought I was crazy for taking the position, and others made comments about my choices without knowing the full story.

The logs you are attempting to jump on will line up, and the hops will become easier—when you stop carrying the weight of what others think.

What they didn't realize was that I was being authentically *me*. From a music therapist in private practice to a school principal, my work in private and public organizations gave me the opportunities I craved for learning and experiencing new fields. Am I less than others because of my path? Or do I add value because of my alternative experiences?

The truth is that every experience, every degree, led me to the place where I am supposed to be. In this work, you really *can't* fake it until you make it, and you may burn out in the process. When you are clear about what you want to do, though, your path will become clear, too. The logs you are attempting to jump on will line up, and the hops will become easier—when you stop carrying the weight of what others think. In this work, you don't have a lot of time to worry about others. Stop overthinking your decisions and what people might think, and do what you have been called to do.

You will only lead well when you *want* to lead from your position and in a way that is authentically you. Public opinion shouldn't get a vote in your next career move. If it does, are you really doing the work you want to do? Or are you manipulating the logs and lily pads to make them take you on the path that others expect of you?

When you have identified your passion, leading forward gets easier. Leading from the classroom, the office, the district, or any other level is more enjoyable when you have made your own decisions, rather than allowing others to make decisions for you. Intentional actions in your career allow for more authentic interactions with those around you. Because I love working with middle school students, I pull into work with a smile on my face and excitement about the opportunity to learn and lead alongside thirteen- and fourteen-year-olds every day. Because of that passion, I am confident in my actions and interactions. I am intentional in my decision to do something I love, and everyone is reaping the benefit of that.

It all starts with authentic grace—and that grace is, ultimately, *your* game. You can play with any rules, and in any way, as long as you have confidence in your decisions and are intentional with your actions.

Honestly, that is part of the fun of leading with authentic grace: you now have permission to play the game the way you want.

LEAD**FORWARD**STRATEGY
Create Your Own Rules

- **Decide on the game.** Who do you want to be when you grow up? Too often, we race through high school and college without really thinking about what we want to do when we grow up. Fast forward to being an adult, and you might feel like you missed out on the chance to think through what you want to do. Journal the big dreams you have for your future, and keep them close. You might be in the exact right place today, or you might be thinking that your life could look different if you took the leap and tried something new. When opportunities present themselves, remind yourself of your big dreams and make sure that when you say yes, you are aligning with the work you want to accomplish. Focus on your thoughts, ideas, and dreams, and get rid of the negative self-talk about what you "think" others will think.

- **Find a way to lead in an area you enjoy.** Living out your joys doesn't always need to equate to a full-time career or job change. Are you a former basketball player? Challenge your students to a game before school. Do you love music? Play at an upcoming school concert. Artist? Work with a group of students to create new artwork in the main office. Take your talents and passions and put them into practice. Crossing your passions over with your current position allows you to share your joys with those around you and might offer a new way to build stronger relationships with them as well.

- **If you don't want someone's advice, don't ask for it.** If you already know in your mind that you are going to say yes or no to an opportunity, quit asking others for their opinions. If you already know you want to apply for that new position, sign up for that 5K, or start a blog, don't seek other people's permission to make those changes in your life. Every step in this life journey is yours to make and take, not for other people to make for you. Stick to your intentions and your idea of who you want to be. Stay the course and be cautious when others' words and opinions attempt to take you off track.

Be Me? Be Better? Be You.

Comparison. Comparison to our colleagues, those we look up to, and the ones we see on social media. It is so hard not to compare ourselves to anyone and everyone, especially when we are working through parts of ourselves that are not clearly defined, or that are hard for us to see and face. You can have a great idea for a new project and shoot it down in your mind before anyone else gets time to hear it. Too often, I make assumptions and jump to conclusions about what others might think, and take time away from my dreams in fear of others' nightmares.

If you have an idea, the only way you will know if it will work is if you share it. Authentic grace means ensuring that your focus is on creating the best version of yourself and what your organization needs, rather than comparing yourself to anyone on any social media platform.

New leaders are in the toughest spot. They have come behind someone who was loved or liked, or who people were glad to see leave. People will expect new leaders to lead in the way others did, even if it wasn't what was good for the school. Without core soft skills like confidence in yourself, you can easily get sucked into those expectations and find yourself reliving someone else's reality instead of creating your own leadership style.

Have you ever been in a new situation or setting when you said something and everyone turned and stared? I call this the whiplash effect. A stakeholder asks a question and I give a response that causes them to do a double-take, as it wasn't the response they were used to getting. They might even come back a few times afterward and ask the same thing, just to make sure they heard me right, and that I didn't change my mind. It would be hard *not* to self-question your decision after that type of reaction, but stick to your vision. It is certainly essential to have deeper conversations on the "why" of how you lead, but you do not need to change how you lead to fit the staff's vision of what it looks like.

Successful school leaders keep their journeys in front of them, and their past successes and experiences in their rearview mirrors as foundations upon which to draw. Leading authentically means learning from your past successes and mistakes, and asserting yourself when you know that something is going to work.

So how do you build those personal leadership skills? How do you know if your vision of leadership is coming across in your practice? Tools like Enneagram, Myers-Briggs Type Indicator (MBTI), and Gallup CliftonStrengths can help you assess and define your style. Take the time to self-assess and reflect on your leadership results and you will start to put your leadership style into daily, intentional practice.

Recently, I took the Enneagram assessment to get a sense of my personality type and whether it is linked to how I thought I was leading in school and life. Within the nine types, I had a two-way tie for my first- and second-highest scores by trait. My top four types were within a point of each other: Loyalist, Helper, Achiever, and Reformer. After completion of the assessment, I spent time reviewing the skills, attributes, and challenges associated with each trait. I was reassured when skills such as hard-working, organized, thoughtful, other-orientated, ambitious, and ethical appeared. However, I wasn't surprised when traits such as anxious, people-pleasing, and image-conscious appeared. And do you know what I did with that information? Pulled it into my style and started intentionally using it in my everyday leadership.

Here's the deal with learning about yourself and your leadership style: it isn't always going to include the things you want to see or hear. But to learn and grow as a leader, you need to know the good and bad things about your style.

After you have defined your leadership style, consider whether what you feel on the inside matches how you lead on the outside. Ask a trusted friend and mentor what leadership characteristics best describe you, and see whether they match what you have identified for yourself. I wrote down key attributes I thought I was reflecting in my leadership style, and then asked around using questions like:

- If you could use one word to describe my leadership style, what would it be?

- How have you seen me live out my servant leadership skills in school?

- I am looking to improve my ability to be vigilant and protective of our initiatives, and ensure we aren't taking on too much as a school. How have you seen that lived out?

- I am trying to improve my skills of being empathetic in parent meetings. After this IEP, can you give me feedback on how I demonstrated this during my interactions with the student and guardian?

Leading with a sense of the attributes you want to be known for requires that you seek honest feedback from others. Leading with an authentic grace means knowing who you are and how you best lead, but it also means allowing others to hold you accountable in that regard. Keep circling back to your core group of trusted colleagues for answers, and then branch out to ask others. Watch how staff members respond when you ask them to give you feedback, and how that one authentic move improves the culture of the school itself.

LEADFORWARDSTRATEGY
Define Your Leadership Style

- **Assess yourself.** Personality and leadership assessments and quizzes give you a sense of how you lead. Taking time to assess and reflect on your style is as important as keeping up with your license and other credentials. Take the quizzes listed earlier to determine your leadership qualities, and start thinking about how you'll incorporate them into your leadership style. What you know is only the first piece of the puzzle. You must also learn to use it when working with others—especially if you're leading them!

- **Put your assessment into practice.** Leadership assessments are not a checkoff or a do/done activity. Once the assessment is complete, review the results and find ways to build up your areas of strength and develop areas where you can improve. Understanding the soft skill of leading during interactions is just as essential as having content knowledge when it comes to leadership.

- **Reflect, review, and set goals.** Are you reviewing site plans and your own leadership goals? Do you want to become a more transformational leader? Would you like to learn how to be a more active listener? Or are you curious about ways to become more adaptable during meetings? Find an area where you can improve, and identify ways to do it. Leadership books, inside and outside of education, can provide clear examples and resources for cultivating the leadership skills and characteristics you need to move your learning forward.

It Is Not a Competition; It Is a Calling

Too often and too early in my career, I continued to compare my journey, faults, and failures against those who came before me. No place was better for this punishment than Facebook. I started using this social media tool in the wrong way. I would watch other leaders post about fun games with their staff, treats in the lounge, and the incredible graphics they created, and instead of feeling inspired, I felt jealous and defeated. I started to doubt my abilities based upon one single picture. How could I ever be the leader the school needed me to be when I wasn't coordinating a Holiday Gift Exchange in the way others were?

Never compare your beginning to another person's end, middle, or any other point in their journey. Seriously, make yourself stop. If you are not entering spaces where people are sharing resources as an opportunity to learn and grow, don't open the app, don't attend the conference, and don't engage in the conversation. Being authentic in your leadership also means admitting you have a lot to learn. And sometimes you are not ready to learn the lesson.

When you are exhausted, overwhelmed, or experiencing a difficult season at school or home, it is okay to pull back. For me, the last two weeks of the school year are my breaking point. Wrapping up one year, planning for the next, staying on top of my kids' spring events, and making summer plans all take an emotional and physical toll on me. Knowing and owning this means I have to be realistic and honest about what has to get done right then, and what can wait. Knowing that allows me to be more efficient, generous, and graceful, and it's all because I've learned to be authentically me when it comes to my boundaries.

Similar to comparison, competition can steal your opportunities to enhance your leadership style while building up those around you. Worrying and wondering about how someone else would do what you are going to do will only delay the delivery of your work and diminish your chances of leading in your authentic way. Just because one teacher delivered a lesson one way doesn't mean you have to do it the same way. In the same breath, if you stop looking up to a mentor and start looking for flaws in their delivery as a way to make yourself feel better about your work, you will end up making yourself feel worse.

In a world that is constantly pushing us to compete and compare ourselves to others, we must find a way to stop and focus on being our personal best.

Start with what you can control: your thoughts. If you are only looking at people's social media feeds to give you a reason to gossip or grumble, stop following them or stop scrolling until you are ready to learn from them instead of hating them. Work to find one positive thing from each post or blog you read, and leave a positive comment. If you start with the positives, the negatives will begin to disappear. In face-to-face interactions, react positively in real time.

You'll be surprised how quickly you go from comparison/competition mode to graceful brainstorming/building-up mode.

Being mindful about how you are entering into interactions and building a collaborative mindset rather than a competitive one will lead you to a whole new world—one where you are learning to grow together.

LEAD**FORWARD**STRATEGY
Create a Clearinghouse

Are you finding and hearing great ideas, but overwhelmed at the thought of implementing them all? Feeling pressured to do that one cool thing you saw on Twitter, but then realizing you already have enough on your plate today to last the rest of the year? Authentic grace in action is all about recognizing that you can learn from others and their interactions without having to copy them or compete. Instead, look for ways to get better at what you're already doing.

- **Make a board.** Do you ever surf the internet for one thing and end up finding a bunch of other ideas you were not necessarily looking for? Create a space to save great ideas to come back to later. I have a Pinterest board titled "Middle School Bucket List." This is a board full of articles, ideas, and activities I find on social media that I want to try in the future. On my Goodreads app, I keep a section for books I want to read by category: for fun, for personal growth, for middle school, for parenting. Then, when I am ready, I have my already curated clearinghouse and don't need Google to tell me what is popular.

Not into Pinterest? Keep a journal or a list somewhere that you can easily reference. I have file folders at school labeled "Summer Work," "Ideas with Ryan" (our assistant principal), and my favorite, "Well these seemed like a good idea on my long run." By archiving and creating space for these ideas, I keep myself from getting overwhelmed by them, but have them ready when I need them. I also don't get down on myself about how much more other people are accomplishing. After all, so much of what they do ends up in my future plans!

- **Create a team.** Let's be honest, leaders need to recognize what we *don't* do well, too. Recognizing that you don't know it all, and don't have all the skills, isn't a weakness; it's an opportunity to lift up others in their leadership abilities and gifts, and to learn from them. Looking at what others are doing and learning from them increases your leadership skills. Do you have a PBIS team? School culture team? Student leadership group? Sunshine Committee? Create a team that helps you work on areas where you need help, and allow yourself to grow.

Reading the Room

Has this happened to you? You walk into a room and start interacting with someone, and things just seem, well, off? You tell a joke and the reaction doesn't bring the response you were expecting. Or maybe you can sense that something is wrong. I call this my gut check—when someone or something just doesn't seem right. Leading with authenticity means utilizing soft skills such as observation to ensure that you are reading the room and the people correctly. If you aren't using these skills, your words and actions might end up being the wrong ones for the situation.

Practicing these skills might mean that the agenda you had in your head must change. Maybe you spend more time on the front end checking in with the staff member who seems off. It might also mean you suspend the agenda until the team is done working through the elephant in the room. But it's well worth it to sacrifice the agenda in favor of making sure the people feel right. Have the confidence to address your people before you address your calendar. Some might call you unconventional or a little off, but the more you lead as your best self, the less you will focus on what others think you should be doing.

A byproduct of this new focus is that it will give you more opportunities for observing others and getting a sense of their daily interactions and actions. Morning supervision is one of my daily routines when it comes to reading the room. I love walking the halls and seeing who is hanging out with whom, which halls are the "hot spots," and the facial reactions to greetings given by peers and staff. One cold, wintery Minnesota morning, I was out with my coat and radio greeting seventh- and eighth-graders as they came into school. Right away, I had a sense that Lea was off. Every day, she and I had the same sort of interaction:

> Me: Waves at Lea as she gets off the bus.
> Lea: Smiles and walks toward me.
> Me: "Lea, how are you today?"
> Lea: "Good. How is your day, Mrs. Cabeen?"
> Me: "Lea, I am great! Thanks again for asking! I tell you, if everyone greeted me like you, I would do this job for free."
> Lea: Smiles, puts AirPods back in, and walks to the school doors.

However, this morning, something was different about Lea. She gave little to no eye contact and walked right by me, AirPods in the whole time. My gut told me something was off. Twenty minutes later, I found her group of friends and asked if everything was okay. Her friends told me her parents were splitting up and she was worried she wouldn't be living with her siblings anymore. After the first hour, I was able to get Lea into the office, and we talked through her sadness and found a counselor to meet with her. The next day, we were back to our routine.

When you are in tune with others, you have multiple gut moments. Maybe someone's smile isn't as big, maybe their "I'm fine" doesn't sound fine. Our students tend to store their emotions on their sleeves, on their faces, and in their actions and interactions with us. As educators, we learn that what students say to us when they are hurt isn't necessarily what they mean. Pushing through that deepens relationships and shows them that we really see them, even when they are hurt.

When you lead these conversations as your authentic self, you are more likely to see the other person pull down their wall and take off the gloves. It's essential to make a personal connection with the other party and then use that to build a foundation for the conversation. Regarding Lea, we also connected on the subject of hair extensions, which we both had. Later on in the year, I again saw her looking agitated. Knowing she liked to use her hands, I said, "Hey, I know how hard those extensions are to get in, and today is not the day I want to see anyone's coming out by force."

That statement, that connection, and honestly the fact that a forty-something-year-old principal made an outlandish statement made Lea stop in her tracks and laugh.

When you use your skills of observation and key into those you serve, you might see when there is more to the story. Take time to ask questions, listen to responses, and let the other person know you care, and you will establish deep relationships. Maybe you are the one person they have talked to, and maybe you can help them find an outlet. Regardless, you will have let them know that they can count on you to truly see them. Leading authentically requires you to practice the skill of assessing your surroundings. Use your gut check to get a sense of who is in the room and how they are feeling. When your gauge is on, you can be confident that your message will come across the way you want it to, and hit the mark.

LEADFORWARDSTRATEGY
Read the Audience

Reading the room requires you to read the people you are serving. When you ensure that your focus is on them instead of on yourself, you speak to the soft skills of intentionality through the caring lens of leadership.

- **Location, location, location.** Be present and engaged in spaces in the school. The best opportunities for leading are the places where people are learning and working. Observations in classrooms, staff meetings, and other spaces give you a chance to see how others interact when they are not on the spot. Practice in hallways and during lunch supervision, when you have access to large numbers of students and individuals in a relatively compact space.

- **Ask a few questions and listen more often.** Wait time—I learned that skill early in my career and continue to apply it at home with my teenage boys. Ask a question and then wait and wait for the answer. Peppering someone with qualifiers and clarifications shifts the conversation from them back to you, and defeats the purpose. Sometimes the first question won't get you to the deep issues, but practice that wait time and listen for clues that might help guide the next question deeper.

- **Phone a friend.** If an interaction seems off with staff members or students, reach out to someone close to them. You may find that someone else has an inside track and cares enough about them to give you some guidance. Taking the time to reach out shows that you can recognize when things are not going according to plan and be willing to ask for help to make them better.

Accountability, Ownership, and Everything in Between

Everything that happens is your responsibility, not your fault. As a driven person, I take on too many tasks and too much owner-ship of others' behaviors and actions. This type of leadership leads to burnout, and ultimately takes ownership away from the right person and puts it on your plate.

Leading with authentic grace means that you assign ownership and accountability to others. For example, let's say parents and staff report concerns about the dismissal plan for students, and that some staff members are not walking their students out to the bus but instead releasing them from the classroom or front door. This is not the plan that the staff agreed upon, nor the way it was reviewed at back-to-school staff meetings and parent conferences. While it isn't your fault that some teachers choose not to follow the plan, it *is* your responsibility to get them on board. A guide to addressing staff who are not engaged in the work as agreed upon could look like this:

1. Observe the situation. Are you seeing it for yourself or going off what others are reporting? Make sure

you are addressing the right thing, and that the other person knows you have seen it. It's important to be present and see the behavior for yourself.

2. Observe for multiple days. This gives you an opportunity to see where the plan is breaking down. Is it the same staff member? Does it happen only on certain days? Observing the situation multiple times can give you a better sense of how to support healthy change. You'll also give yourself a chance to find the right way to assert your leadership, since you'll have specifics rather than just a vague idea.

3. Ask questions. This is a great way to ensure that you fully understand the intent of what's going on. Make sure you ask the question in the right way and at the right time. Going up to a staff member in front of their students as they are leaving doesn't give them time to formulate a response, and calls them out in front of those they serve.

Next, talk to those teachers specifically. I don't recommend the "spray and pray" approach to change. If you just tell everyone to walk their kids to the bus, the ones already doing so will continue, but feel unnecessary pressure. And if the other staff members didn't hear it before in full staff meetings, why would they now? If they did hear it and chose not to listen, chances are good that they'll continue to make that choice. Meet them at their door at dismissal and walk with them, modeling hugs, high-fives, and waves to parents as you walk ... all the way ... with their class. Reinforce this behavior when you see it and directly communicate with specific people if they continue to refuse to follow building practices.

What if a colleague continues to "sneak" into the building late and asks you not to tell on them? If it is an occasional ask, let it go. When it becomes a pattern, address it directly. Say things like, "Brooke, when you are late it impacts the safety of our students and takes away our team time as we are waiting for your insight and input." And report (not tattle) the concerns to a supervisor. Don't take their behavior on as your fault or your problem. Be authentic rather than beating around the bush or avoiding the confrontation, and show them what you expect of them.

LEAD**FORWARD**STRATEGY
Address It, Deal with It, Then Move On

Asserting your leadership with soft skills means you sometimes have to take it slow. Instead of brushing off or passing over a situation, take the time to address it.

- **Write it down.** What is bothering you about the interaction or circumstance? Take the time to mind dump the entire situation to help get to the root of the issue, and it will make addressing it more intentional. Think about the following prompts:

    - What happened?

    - What was said?

    - What was secondhand information?

    - How do I feel?

    - Why is this bothering me so much?

- **Practice.** Conflict is not on anyone's list of favorite things to do at work. The only way we can get through it is to get better at it. Read up on strategies for addressing conflict, and find a style that best fits you. Before you go off sending the message or interacting, practice with a colleague or a supervisor, or if needed, a human resource director and/or union representative. Better preparation will help you get through it more authentically and with more intention—and will reap a better result for you and whomever you're speaking with.

• **Reflect.** After having a conversation, seek feedback from a neutral party or circle back to the partner after the interaction. What could you have done better? Was the message clear? Did you miss anything? Ask questions to help you improve your strategies and you'll show others that this skill is a work in progress and that you believe it is important.

Not Perfect, But Purposeful

Building the leadership trait of vulnerability and owning my novice status required me to be transparent not only about how I lead, but about the chances of success on my first attempts. If you were to ask any staff member at Ellis Middle School what I was shooting for during my first year as the leader, they could all tell you that I wanted to be accurate 73 percent of the time.

Now, I have no idea how I chose 73 percent, but I shared this goal at the first staff meeting, and it stuck. I told everyone immediately that the last time I worked at the middle school level, Facebook was getting popular and students were just starting to switch from flip phones to smart ones. Welcome to 2019, Mrs. Cabeen. As my transition from kindergarten to seventh and eighth grade happened eight weeks before the school year started, I needed to be honest with the staff. I only knew a fraction of what I needed to know regarding practical application, but I had a willingness to learn and a ton of attributes from previous leadership assessments that told me I could do it. I had to be honest; this staff was not getting a Pinterest Perfect Principal. But I was going to try my best to be the best for them.

I was a little scared at being that authentic with people who had just hired me to lead their school. Would they race to the central office right after the meeting and ask them to send me packing? Could my honesty put some people off, or make them less confident in my abilities? Fast forward to the second semester, though, and the outcomes our school, students, and staff were producing exceeded my 73 percent accurate-the-first-time rating I had set at the start of the school year! I never promised to be perfect in my leadership, but I guaranteed I would be intentional in my focus to accomplish our goals—and I would do it with the help of the entire team.

LEADFORWARDSTRATEGY
Lead with Intention

Leading well isn't about perfection, but about execution. Knowing exactly what your goal is and finding creative ways to hit the target in your authentic style shows your willingness to learn, grow, and do good for those you serve.

- **Find a target and keep it in sight.** As you transition from one year to the next, set two to three goals for yourself and have measurable outcomes. Benchmark your progress and share the results with stakeholders to keep yourself and your leadership goals present throughout the year.

- **Share success.** Too often, we spend more time talking about what we did wrong than what went right. Don't be afraid to share with others how your authentic way of doing the work is making a difference with those you serve. Go out of your way to make appointments specifically for this purpose every week, and remember to spread the love. Don't only talk about yourself; include the ways the team is moving forward together.

- **Post your goals.** In my office, I have an 8-by-10 piece of paper hanging up that posts the Site and Principal Goals. At the end of each quarter, I put together a spreadsheet to review progress on each goal and report to specific audiences about it. This goes right back to sharing the success, as I said earlier, because it gives me a specific format in which to do just that, and makes sure that I keep all interested parties in the conversation. Having visible goals keeps them in focus all year and helps me remain on the right path, while sharing them with others holds me accountable.

MOVING**FORWARD**

Too often, incredible educators, paraprofessionals, administrative assistants, and future leaders doubt whether they can impact others. Why do they doubt this? Because they don't have a title in front of or behind their name. Too few people—who could be incredible leaders—are sharing their stories, including their voices, and applying for new opportunities because they think they are not worthy.

The future principal said, "I don't think I could lead like you." My response: "You shouldn't. Leading with authenticity means you lead like you, not like anyone else."

But leading with grace and authenticity doesn't require a title.

When I am in a room full of amazing people and this comes up, I ask, "If not you, then who?" If you have a passion to start an after-school club for students, do it. If you want to start visiting students and families in the home, go for it. If you have aspired to become a leader in a new position, apply for it. Being authentic in your work and word takes brave action. The more often you try, the less scary it will be.

I had a recent conversation with an aspiring principal about what leadership looks like, and the future principal said, "I don't think I could lead like you." My response: "You shouldn't. Leading with authenticity means you lead like you, not like anyone else." Find your fit and run with it. Greet your class at the door, spend time in the lunchroom, sit with families at concerts and sporting events, and start making Good News Calls of the Day. Whatever you choose to do, do it with intention and your unique take on it. The more meaningful it is for you, the more meaningful it will be for those who receive it. Continue to seek resources for learning more about how you lead best. What meetings, committees, or relationships are the best places for you to start this journey? How will you intentionally reflect on leading as your best self? And who can hold you accountable in this work?

By answering these questions, you will ensure that even when you change directions mid-leap, you will still be heading for the right destination. And finally, when you feel like you are not making progress or are even going backward, ask yourself: How am I taking a step back to get a running leap forward?

CHAPTER 1
LEADFORWARDJOURNAL

My authentic path

Map out my path. Write down where I started my career, and mark all the stops along the way until I get to my present-day position.

_____

_____

_____

_____

_____

_____

Reflect and identify one leadership trait I developed while I was on each log in my *Frogger* journey.

_____

_____

_____

_____

_____

I am who I say I am

What three words define my leadership style?

_____

_____

_____

Use each word in a sentence describing how I lead authentically.

_____

_____

_____

_____

_____

_____

Reflect: How can I live out these characteristics every day in small ways?

_____

_____

_____

_____

_____

_____

_____

_____

_____

Share your journal entries and ideas at #LeadForward on Twitter.

CHAPTER 2

Vulnerable Grace

Give It Your Best, Even When
You Are at Your Worst

In order to rise, you have to lay your burden down.
— SALLY HELGESEN AND MARSHALL GOLDSMITH,
AUTHORS OF *HOW WOMEN RISE*

EADING WITH VULNERABILITY means letting go of the perception that you have to lead with perfection. Becoming comfortable in your imperfection and talking about it with others is an opportunity to establish authentic relationships, rather than those built with a Facebook filter that only shows the good, and none of the bad.

Just because you are the leader doesn't mean you don't have a lot to learn. I wish I would have known this when I started my career. I spent years, and lots of tears, thinking I should do it all in isolation, without help and support. And as a woman in leadership, I felt even more lonely and guilty, and I missed many opportunities to build bridges with those around me and grow a network of learners and leaders that would help equip me to do the work. Instead, I let my pride prevail and worked alone for years.

Throughout this chapter, we will work through the idea that to lead, you must do a lot of learning along the way. And that learning is going to be messy. You are going to make mistakes for which you'll probably have to apologize. The journey is imperfect— and totally worth it.

Novice Versus Expert

There is a huge lie in leadership. I am not sure where it started, but I see it in all organizations and with both new and seasoned leaders. The lie: You need to lead like an expert. Some people lead like they believe they know what they are talking about, while their audience knows they know nothing about the topic. I call these people "Surface Leaders." They know a little about a lot but talk like they have a PhD in everything. They walk into a meeting dressed in their suits, with their tech tools and gadgets. Their networking consists of name-dropping and reminders of who they are and what their title is, just in case you forgot in the last five minutes. If you receive an email from them, the bio after their signature is longer than the email contents!

Watch these leaders try to lead a meeting. They start out strong, saying the right words and quoting the right people. But in the follow-up, they lose their ground. When asked to explain a tool or a strategy they just brought up, they say things like, "Well, in my reading, this is what it says" or "Well, (name) told me it is like this." If you can, watch the audience react and respond to this type of leader. Around this time, their heads go down, they engage in sidebar conversations, or worse yet, they check out and retreat into their own narrative and start mentally preparing to leave. We all have experienced this type of leadership, and many of us have tried to lead in this manner as well.

Recognize that to lead well, you need to listen and learn more often than you thought necessary. This is an essential soft skill when it comes to building a culture of trust, commitment, and responsibility.

An example of this learning in action is my most recent transition back to middle school. In two years, I went from two different schools, and from 400 kindergartners to 750 seventh- and eighth-graders. Before this jump, I had spent six years learning and understanding the developmental value of play, data meetings, and PLC topics that drove instruction and collaboration in kindergarten. Moving back to middle school meant I had to gain that confidence in a whole new realm. I had been away from middle school for seven years, and things had changed. Schedules were different, and state assessments were now done online (i.e., no more paper/pencil bubble assessments and protocols). I was way out of my league and had no chance of leading with the confidence I had left from the kindergarten setting.

While I was preparing to interview for the position, I considered all I would have to learn and the skills I was lacking. I knew I was walking into an interview to speak to a group in a setting I had no experience in, and that I would struggle to immediately relate to.

So what did I do? I told the truth. During the interview, I shared my vulnerability. I reframed my status as a novice in this age group as a strength rather than a weakness. I said that I was not an expert, but that my previous experience and growth mindset would be positive attributes. I said that my lack of knowledge would encourage me to rely on the knowledge of my team, which would allow me to build relationships with stakeholders. I explained that the way I learned best was by being in the halls, classrooms, and other spaces where I could build relationships and my knowledge.

In that interview, I used the skills I had built in other principalships as leverage. While in the primary setting, I had learned the power of sharing our school story on social media, and had noticed that middle schools could use that skill to increase their positive presence for families. After three years of leading with an incredible PLC team and staff, I could bring the framework to the middle school and establish a team model for daily relationship-building and intentional conversations with staff. As the leader of the school that was the entry point of the K–12 setting, I learned how to answer questions in a way that supported a trusted relationship, and how to navigate difficult conversations and build a sense of belonging with all families.

It was my final skill set that I was most excited about sharing with this interview committee of seasoned middle school educators. I was coming with six years of kindergarten experience, *and* with a knowledge of the next six years of incoming middle schoolers to this school! Yes, after one year, the following six would be the students I'd had at the kindergarten center. And anyone who has worked at a middle school knows how valuable that experience is.

Mostly, I allowed myself to be vulnerable and to admit that I would need help in the spots I couldn't handle on my own. Framing my vulnerability with the expertise I could bring showed the team, and myself, that I didn't need to speak the title, but lead with authenticity and vulnerability.

Leading with vulnerability requires a significant amount of laughter.

Fast forward six months into this new position. I really can't make this up. So far this year, we have had ten snow days—a delay into the third quarter by at least three days. A full day of no phones or internet. Snowblowers on our roof during the day due to a large amount of snow, a day when the bells just wouldn't stop ringing, and most recently, a fire alarm going off fifteen minutes before the school day started. Yes, you read that right: just as students were walking into school, a frozen sprinkler triggered an alarm that called the fire department and had us evacuating in the middle of a winter that just wouldn't end. Teachers who have taught the majority of their careers in this building had never seen a year like this one.

I could have called in sick and hidden under the covers on any of these occasions. I could have placed blame or targeted others, but instead, I named it, owned it, and coined it. Leading with vulnerability means that even when you do not have all the answers, you have to own up to the questions in your unique way. As a leader, you can't control everything that happens, but you can orchestrate your response and keep your vision in view, no matter how many detours you end up taking.

Leading with vulnerability requires a significant amount of laughter. You may not be able to control all the circumstances that occur while you are leading, but you can certainly control your response to them. Own it and lead with it, not in spite of it. Trust me; it is easier to acknowledge the elephant in the room instead of trying to cover it up or pretend it just doesn't exist.

Simply stated, I owned my novice status. I didn't try to brush it under the rug, but I put it right on the table. I was honest and proud of the fact that I had a lot to learn and I wanted to learn it with the staff, students, and families I was honored to serve. And how did that go for me? I am living and leading at that school while preparing for my first class of kindergarten students to walk through the door as seventh-graders in six short months. I am prepared for the next frozen sprinkler, day without internet, and anything else that might come our way. Leading with vulnerability means you don't need to have all the answers, but you do need a willingness to roll with whatever gets thrown your way. Having honest conversations, sharing your worries and mistakes, and learning with and from your team will provide a foundation for a strong school culture.

LEAD**FORWARD**STRATEGY
Own Your Novice Status

These are the hard things we don't always learn in our leadership classes. Instead of focusing so much on how we must be perfect, let's start figuring out how to be *present*. When you enter the classroom, office, or any other space, be willing to own your mistakes, and be honest about what you know and what you don't.

- **Try something new.** Don't forget that we were all students before we were what we are now. If we're being honest, we're *still* all students of something! Take a learner's mindset when leading with vulnerability. Sub in a class outside your content comfort zone, implement a new strategy in the classroom, and play a game with your students. Regularly tackling and taking risks shows others and yourself that leading and learning go hand in hand.

- **Don't reinvent the wheel.** Many times, you can find great ideas right around the corner in another classroom or nearby school. And you can learn something in the process. Is another school or classroom doing a cool project? Don't try to outdo their idea; instead, ask if you can use it. Leading like a newbie gives you opportunities to ask others for help and ideas, and has the added benefit of getting you involved with others and building your personal network.

- **Laugh about it.** Seriously, don't take yourself so seriously. One way of owning your mistakes is to laugh about them and learn from them. Allow yourself to be human, and you will model for students and staff that it is okay for them to try, regardless of whether they succeed or fail.

- **Learn from it.** It is okay to try something … and then never, ever do it again. In the past year, I have tried great activities and initiatives that we will do again next year. We had about the same number of activities that failed miserably! Mistakes are great ways to build background knowledge for future experiences.

It's Not About Us, It's About Them: Learning to Ask for Help

I am always cautious about how I introduce myself. I often enter new situations as an "educator," because I don't want my title or accomplishments to cloud anyone's idea that I am truly a learner. At times, it catches people off guard, including my students. One day I was in an eighth grade language arts class and the topic of social media came up. Since these middle schoolers still believe I grew up without electricity and running water, they decided they'd better give me a tutorial on Twitter. Until they looked me up. "Wow, Cabeen, you are, like, famous?!" was the response from one of my students. Suddenly my street cred went up with him and his friends.

Well, I should say it went up for about three minutes—until I asked how to take a selfie. "Cabeen, you don't know how to take a real selfie?" he questioned. Confused, I showed him what I was trying to do, and it proved that I didn't know what I was doing. That day, in that class, I took my first selfie with the volume button on my cell phone. The student and I posted that picture on Twitter and then circled back later to see how many people liked it. This underscores an important fact: your followers, your success, and your accomplishments are secondary to the fact that you can always grow and learn from others—even eighth grade boys. This realization is essential to leading with grace and learning from your vulnerabilities.

Lesson learned: be honest and ask for opinions and help. When you don't have to worry about what others think, you have more time to plan and execute the vision you are trying to achieve. Instead of overthinking and underestimating the willingness of others to help, try asking. A good rule to remember: never walk into an opportunity to gain feedback with something you are confident is 100 percent accurate. With any proposal, site plan, or building goals document, I shoot for that 73 percent certainty that I have a finished product. Whatever the task, I come with the outline or the big vision and timeline, and then we work together to ensure that we didn't overlook or overthink any aspect. Our teams leave feeling empowered and excited, and I feel more confident in the final product because it went through multiple trials and gained multiple perspectives and insights.

As a building leader, it is impossible to know the intricate details in all aspects of the school. However, you do need to know who the key stakeholders are, and whether they will give you honest feedback and fill in the cracks. Have the grace and vulnerability to not only ask for feedback but to follow through with it.

LEADFORWARDSTRATEGY
Be Honest and Ask for Opinions and Help

This is not the time, place, or space to try to fake it until you make it. Owning your inexperience and asking for help early on will help you grow, and help your team go further sooner than if you had tried to fake your way through the situation. So how do you go about finding the right team and feedback?

- **Find a network.** Developing vulnerability in leadership takes time and people who you trust, respect, and admire. Who is that student, parent, or teacher that will help you stay accountable to yourself and point out areas of growth? Surround yourself with people who represent the different stakeholders you serve. Ask for their opinions, and then listen to them.

- **Be specific.** When asking for help, be detailed about what type of feedback you are looking for from the other person. Are you worried you are not being clear? Concerned that the message is getting lost? Or are you a little on the long-winded side? When you want feedback, be specific about what you are looking for so the other person can look for exactly what you need.

- **Be grateful.** Nothing means more in this work than incorporating sincere manners and social graces. Circle back and thank the other person for their feedback. The more you ask for help and for others' time and advice, the more you grow and get support in return, but make sure you're being appropriately thankful for the help. A phone call, a PM, a thank-you card, a coffee meeting … the possibilities are endless, and each one will help you deepen the relationship—and ensure that you can go to that person for help again in the future!

The Illusion of the Skinny Mirror

I have an obsession with skinny mirrors. When I need to get a new mirror for a space in our home or school office, I will line them up and look at myself in each one to see which makes me look "skinny." My husband just knows to walk away for a while if I am at Target lining them all up and walking back and forth in front of them. Then I will spend time figuring out the best place to mount the mirror in the space. I can even tell you which stores have better skinny mirrors than others. For some reason, after looking in a skinny mirror, I have an instant boost of confidence. I will immediately experience a good hair day and a coordinated outfit, and even start thinking my ankles look better. This obsession also rolls into the workplace. I catch myself checking out different mirrors, and know which ones are the best in any building that I regularly go into. When I would be having a moment in our old school, the secretary would tell me to go to Lori's room and look in the skinny mirror, knowing that I needed a little confidence boost to get through the day.

The problem with skinny mirrors is that they only work when you are in front of them. Once you step away, you are back to your old self. I tended to doubt myself without this security blanket. However, what I have also learned is that my perception of who I am outside of the mirror doesn't always match what others think of me. When I thought I was too harsh, others have said I was still kind. When I thought I didn't communicate clearly enough, others disagreed and stated that it wasn't that I didn't communicate clearly, it was that others didn't want to hear what I had to say. My skinny mirror was a way to beat myself up more than I needed to, as I had a distorted perception not only of what I looked like, but of what others thought of me.

This lens has carried with me into many moments of my leadership journey. I often revert to hidden fears and perceptions that are not clear or even a point of focus for others. To move out of that negative mindset, I have learned to ask others for honest and timely feedback in my most vulnerable areas—the ones I needed my skinny mirror to get through.

Sometimes school discussions and decisions require union

representation or central office support, and I have taken those opportunities to ask for feedback before and after the interaction. I will explain what I am going to say and ask for feedback on my verbal and physical appearance during the interaction. Then I make mental notes of what I am learning.

When I first started asking for this feedback, I learned a lot more about who I was rather than what the skinny mirror was telling me. For example, during meetings in which expulsion or significant disciplinary action was pending, what I perceived as nervous energy (i.e., me talking too much or too fast) came across as true sincerity and sensitivity to the situation. The skinny mirror (and my dependence on it) was misleading me about how others saw me.

When working on staff improvement, I also learned that I deliver information, well ... well. My skinny mirror was telling me any "bad" information could never be seen as good in my delivery. Union leadership and teachers who were involved told me, though, that I shared concerns in a caring way and offered ways to work together to solve them. I also learned that other leaders don't always ask for this feedback, and some needed it more than I did. We need to allow ourselves to be vulnerable enough to take feedback, but we also need to accept that feedback can be positive rather than negative.

We need to stop letting the skinny mirror dictate how we lead.

LEAD**FORWARD**STRATEGY
Stop Hiding, Start Looking

I hope you can also quit focusing on finding the skinny mirror (or whatever you use as an equivalent crutch) and start finding ways to be comfortable in the skin you are in. Vulnerable grace is a way to be your best self, whether or not you have a good hair day or are unsure about your outfit. The more we hide who we are, the less we allow others to learn and lead with the real us. Having these honest conversations builds the soft skills necessary to lead through the tough waters.

- **Ask for feedback.** Be specific. When entering a meeting, ask a person who is not directly involved to observe your specific concerns and share what they heard/saw afterward. Take the feedback on board and learn from it. Every time.

- **Record yourself.** With permission, record yourself at a staff meeting. Alternatively, even record yourself practicing what you are going to say in an upcoming difficult conversation. Watch it and look for facial tics and inflections in your voice, and tweak your delivery before you share it in real time. Stop the instant replay in your head of what you think you look like in the mirror, and start to focus on the real picture in front of you—the one that you can see.

- **Get rid of the mirror.** Make sure your idea of yourself is a true picture of what others see. Stop being self-deprecating and doubting your ideas and dreams because others might not like them, or might not agree with you. Too often, we make assumptions about what others think of us. We discount our dreams or refuse to tell others about them because we assume they'll downplay us. Don't let your narrative of who you think you are drown out what others actually see and say about you.

Don't Doubt Yourself

I can still remember the first anonymous feedback survey I received. While about 98 percent of the feedback was positive and constructive, I was stuck on the one comment that wasn't. Someone said

I didn't dress professionally enough. In this new position, I had changed my wardrobe to be more hands-on as a leader and more approachable as a principal. Wearing skirt suits and mostly black didn't hold up well at recess duty and sitting crisscross applesauce during morning meetings. So I had slowly phased out suits for dress pants, jackets, and the occasional leggings and sweater combo. And then this comment came out. I was hurt and embarrassed, and even though 98 percent of the comments were helpful in my growth as a leader, I focused on that one. So I went into our basement and the back of a closet, and pulled out those suits and skirts.

The first day I put on my "old skin" and walked into the school, I sort of felt like I was in a costume, and I also felt a little defeated and hurt. Who I wanted to be wasn't being received well by .1 percent of the school, and I had decided to focus on that rather than on the other 99.9 percent who likely hadn't thought critically about my attire. I was out that morning greeting families at the parent drop-off in one of those "more professional" suits when a paraprofessional I respected and admired approached me. She simply stated, "I liked your other outfits better. This just doesn't fit you."

Suddenly perspective hit me: I will never be 100 percent perfect or 100 percent right in everyone's eyes, but the moment I veer from the way I want to lead because of .1 percent of the audience is the moment when I stop being myself.

When have you changed your course because you were afraid of what that .1 percent would say in a survey, behind your back, or to your face? Think about that staff meeting, that conversation on the team, or that interaction with a parent who is frustrated with you, the school, or a teacher. If you are easily swayed based upon others' opinions, how can you stand firm and tall in what you know needs to be done and in a way that is most authentically you? The more you stand up as your best self, the less time you will spend on self-doubt and worry about the .1 percent. Becoming stronger in your vulnerability requires you to set a boundary between what information and feedback are beneficial … and what are spiteful or mean-spirited.

LEADFORWARDSTRATEGY
Don't Listen to the Comments
from the Cheap Seats

Too often we sit and stew on the feedback that isn't informative, but *is* full of criticism. In doing so, we miss the messages from people we trust. You need to choose those who care for you and want to see you grow, and hold them away from the noise of those who don't. This is an essential skill when it comes to successfully navigating vulnerability in productive ways.

- **Be wary of the naysayers.** Whatever you call them, we all have them. The person who always complains, the one who never has anything positive to say, or the one who will admire a problem instead of looking for ways to solve it. Getting caught up in that pit of negativity will make you lose the broader perspective. Identify the naysayers in your life and start to filter out their comments. Put more weight on comments from the people you trust and respect to help drown out the negative noise.

- **Don't put too much weight on anonymous surveys.** If people can't say it to your face, but can type pages about it without their names, be careful how much time and attention you pay to it. Leading with vulnerability means finding ways not to let unkind, unproductive, and downright mean statements derail what you have been called to do. Find a mentor or a person in your PLN and ask them if what was said anonymously is something that the majority feel. Regardless of the weight of the words, if the comment takes you off course from the vision you have set your sights on, delete and dismiss it and keep moving forward.

- **They make suggestions; you make decisions.**
Remember why you chose this work, and why someone chose you to lead. Just because others don't like it doesn't mean you shouldn't do it. Change is hard, and sometimes feedback is a fear-based response to change. Yes, feedback is essential, but ultimately *you* are the one who decides how, why, and when you lead. If someone shares something, say thank you, and instead of debating, arguing, or disagreeing, just let it be. Remind yourself that whoever is giving you suggestions is not in your shoes. They may not have all the information or see the situation from the view you have. Don't judge their comments, but know that you don't have to jump in and do what they say, either. Take a moment to journal about the suggestion, brainstorm the idea with your PLN, and decide whether it has merit. If it does, draw up a plan for how to introduce it in your goals. If it doesn't, delete it and move on.

Fail Forward

At what age did making a mistake become a flaw? We encourage our children to learn by trying, doing, and learning from errors on assignments. We set reminders that success comes from past failures, but as adults, making mistakes in our day-to-day operations is considered a fault. Too often, we beat ourselves up for small mistakes and miss the opportunity to keep trying and learning. The fear of another fault coming out keeps our mouths shut and our ideas quiet. The best example is on social media. I watch people post great ideas and quotes from their learning, only to be shamed for using incorrect spelling or grammar. People are quick to correct others and slow to find meaning from the message, errors and all. I worry about the voices in our field that are silenced after that one reply or response. So I keep posting, flaws and all. If someone corrects my grammar, I say thank you and leave the post up. If I can't model making mistakes and moving forward, how will others know it is okay to do the same?

We have minute-by-minute opportunities to make mistakes and laugh about them. I think of a recent incident when a situation came up suddenly and I had to make a quick all-school announcement. What you need to know is that I hate getting on the intercom. If I have to say something on that terrible device, I usually have it typed up, take two deep breaths, and place a garbage can next to me in case my nerves take over. Well, that day I had no time to prepare or plan what I needed to say. I just had to do it that second. So in true form, I botched the message. I don't remember exactly what I had to say, but what came out was: "The alarm might trip again as we flush one thing out." Now, in a building of 780 middle school students, this went right over their heads. But the staff ... well, all day people were checking on me to make sure I had "flushed that thing out." A staff member even videoed my freakout—me waving my arms during the announcement in a poor attempt to sound cool and calm on the mic, and the subsequent reaction when I saw I'd been filmed the whole time. That night I even received a few texts and memes about my flushing.

I could have gotten worked up or mortified at the attention, but I found a way to just laugh. I learned the importance of taking ten seconds to write down what I needed to say—next time. As for this incident, I just needed to take a breather and let it go!

Don't tell me you haven't been there. You said the wrong thing in a meeting, you tweeted something that was misspelled, you shared or spoke incorrectly about data in a meeting while sharing a PowerPoint. You missed a cue or your line in a staff skit, you slipped on the ice in front of a parent ... I could go on and on, but you get the idea. Regardless of the mistake, don't stop making them! The only way we get better is by trying and taking risks. Sometimes those risks are easily worth the reward and they work the first time. In other situations, your face might turn a little red, and you might cringe when you think of that moment, but I bet you learned something from the experience, and those around you saw a new side of you as well.

As we have learned in this chapter and in these stories, leading with vulnerability builds essential soft skills that enhance the culture of whatever school you are leading. Moving forward with an honest, caring style and your authentic personality allows you to be present in any context and ready to serve others—while still being open to learning from your mistakes and failing forward. The risk is always worth the reward.

LEAD**FORWARD**STRATEGY
Be Your Best Critic

When we focus on learning from our falls, they don't hurt as much. Being our own best critic and seeing life through a lens of vulnerability means we are ready to learn from our mistakes. Seek this as a learning opportunity, not a fault or flaw in your character.

- **Favor your falls.** Try hard to see good and growth from your mistakes. Before freaking out or running away from a public mistake, stop and take stock of what you could learn. I can honestly tell you I now expect to always spell correctly on social media, after a few flaming/shaming comments. I am also closer to a few people because they took the time to alert me to a misstep that others wouldn't address. Finding the good in your falls allows you to grow, learn, and be better at what you do.

- **Forgive yourself.** We get bruised enough by others in this work; we don't need to do it to ourselves. When something happens, articulate the error, say you are sorry, and then move forward. The more regrets and faults we find in ourselves, the less likely we are to keep trying and taking risks. Allow yourself to make mistakes—and then laugh and learn from them. Don't restrict yourself to the idea of perfection, as it will restrict you from growth as well.

- **Follow up with others.** How often do you take the time to apologize to your students for mistakes you make? I continue to apologize to my students for my mistakes, and seek forgiveness every day. Sometimes it is immediate, while other times it takes a few weeks. Regardless of the timing, the relationships strengthen because I took the time to recognize my misstep, own it, and articulate it to the other party. Have a script ready for this, so that you don't forget to say something or overstate your purpose. Sit down, write it out, and then practice it until you can deliver it without hesitation.

The Art of an Apology

My first year into the assistant principalship, I thought I knew it all (insert eye roll). More accurately, within the first month of the job, I thought I had it all figured out. Students would get sent to the office, I would follow the Rights and Responsibilities document, issue a consequence, contact the parents, rinse, and repeat. Although we had these processes in place, my head and heart were searching for a more restorative way of resolving conflict. I had started reading books and articles on the power of an apology and wanted to try it.

Unfortunately for me, I picked the worst situation to practice it on. When I talk about the teacher with the most patience, care, grit, and perseverance for students, it will always be Mrs. Huffman. She had high expectations, clear standards, and a level of care for her kids that was virtually impossible to replicate in any other sixth grade class. In hindsight, if I had only spent more time observing how she worked with students, rather than reading books, I would have had a practical approach to effectively working with middle schoolers. A month into school, she sent a young man down to the office for disrespect and insubordination, which had been building for a few weeks and damaging the culture of the class.

I read the referral and spoke with the student, and then we walked back (yes, still during the hour) to the class, where he offered an apology. I had him go right back into the class he had been asked to leave. I walked out thinking I had checked off all the boxes of the process I had read about in my research. What I forgot was to ensure that the process was mutually agreed upon, not just thrown at the teacher.

Leading with vulnerability means that at times, we have to peel back the onion and let others see how sincere we are when we misstep.

Shortly after that, the principal came into my office and let me know that I had hurt Mrs. Huffman with my action, and how, in the bigger picture, she rarely ever asked a student to leave the class, and when she did it was for an incredibly good reason. Immediately,

I felt terrible. How could I have done this? Would she hate me forever? Maybe she would never talk to me again, or think I was the worst assistant principal in the history of assistant principals.

Before I went too far in my shaming thoughts, I made time to go down to her classroom after school and apologize. I didn't have a template or framework back then to use when apologizing. All I knew was I had made a big mistake and I wanted to fix it. I don't remember how I said it, but I know it was sincere and I know I teared up a bit. I told her how much I respected her, how much the students in her class learned from her, and how disappointed I was in myself for not understanding the full situation before I made my efficient decision that was not effective at all.

A big sorry to Rachel Hollis and her book *Girl Stop Apologizing*, but sometimes we need to apologize. A true apology is free of "but" or "if you would have." Apologies are specific, honest, and sincere. And they are hard. Leading with vulnerability means that at times, we have to peel back the onion and let others see how sincere we are when we misstep. Stop thinking of mistakes as career-ending and think of them as career-building. Looking back, many of my biggest mistakes led to my best learning moving forward.

What happened next: Mrs. Huffman forgave me. Really, she didn't hold it over me and to this day we are friends and tend to tell the story now with a laugh. She loves to tell others how she taught me how to lead, and I can't disagree. She taught me the importance of making mistakes—and how to fix them.

LEADFORWARDSTRATEGY
How to Apologize Well

- **Be timely.** Don't wait for months or years to say something you could say today. If you have that feeling in your gut that you should say something, lean into that feeling and just do it. My favorite mantra in this situation is to rip it off like a Band-Aid. It has to be done, and the sooner you start, the sooner you finish.

- **Be sincere.** Say it how you mean it, with no hidden agenda. I practice my apologies if at all possible, making sure I don't use "but" or "if only." If you're going to apologize, it means you need to fully own what you did. No qualifiers allowed.

- **Be patient.** You might be ready to seek forgiveness, but that doesn't mean the receiver is ready to accept it. It is okay to state in the apology that at this time the other person doesn't need to say anything. Don't force a response; just wait until they are ready to deliver it, and really listen.

- **Move forward.** Once you ask for forgiveness, it permits you to let go of the guilt of the situation. Quit beating yourself up or bringing the situation up. Learning from your mistakes means moving forward rather than carrying the guilt of the situation with you.

MOVING**FORWARD**

You would think that since I am writing this book, it means I'm comfortable using all the strategies I suggest. Truth: some days, I am afraid to try to do the right thing. Recently, I noticed a student giving me the "stink eye" in the hall and making comments under her breath. I hadn't had direct interactions with her, but I'd had some tough conversations with a few members of her peer group in the past month. Those situations had been resolved, but somehow, she still harbored hurt feelings. At lunch one day, I finally ripped off the Band-Aid and asked to meet with her in the hallway. I asked what I had done for her to be so upset with me. I explained that while, from her perspective, she might think I was always "out to get" her group, but I was really trying to keep everyone safe. I shared a few examples of things I knew or saw that she didn't realize I was aware of and dealing with.

Once I finished, I waited for her to roll her eyes again, argue, or just walk away. Instead, she started crying. She opened up about her hard life at home, and how she had been taking it out on me for no real reason. She apologized for her actions. "Mrs. Cabeen, you really haven't done a thing to me. I am just so mad that I tend to take it out on those around me who care."

Wow.

Going with my gut, I was able to dig more deeply into surface interactions that I could have ignored. We talked about supports for school and home, and I offered her a space to talk whenever she needed. The next day when we passed in the hall, I got a half-smile.

I could share many stories about how I led and leaned in awkwardly, but in the end, it worked. Sometimes the one thing we need to do is the one thing we don't want to do: admit our faults, our role in the argument, or honestly ask what in the world happened for these interactions to be harsh and difficult.

Becoming a leader who builds the vulnerability muscle also means we decrease the use of shame in our thoughts. Stop personalizing mistakes as fatal flaws, and start treating them as learning opportunities. Balance out the awkwardness of the apology with the possibility of strengthening relationships and communication skills. Take away the thoughts about fatal flaws and replace them with intentions to learn and lead as an imperfect person willing to learn and grow every day. Grace and vulnerability in leadership mean making mistakes, owning them, and learning from them moving forward.

CHAPTER 2
LEADFORWARDJOURNAL

Getting real about myself and my leadership style

In what ways have I shared my fears or worries with others?

_____

_____

_____

_____

When have I tried something new and how did it work for me?

_____

_____

_____

_____

What are my three leadership goals for the year?

_____

_____

_____

Where do I post these and how often do I review them?

_____

_____

_____

_____

GOAL: Post my goals on my wall and set calendar appointments for three, six, and nine months from now to review and update my wall.

Learning to say I'm sorry

What have I messed up recently that I know I need to repair?

_____

_____

_____

_____

_____

Write down what I want to say, read it, and practice it out loud. Taking time to practice and prepare will show the other person how much this matters to me.

_____

_____

_____

_____

_____

_____

Share your journal entries and ideas at #LeadForward on Twitter.

Grace with Empathy

Lead Without Judgment and with Understanding

Empathy is not connecting to an experience, it's connecting to the emotions that connect to an experience.
— BRENÉ BROWN, AUTHOR OF *DARE TO LEAD*

Lead Where You Live

REMEMBER IT WELL. I was out in the community and it happened. I ran into a former employee whose departure didn't end well. My first reaction, honestly, was to turn and run. I started to feel my heart race and I tried my best to divert my eyes. The conversations and interactions leading up to the termination left both of us reeling from things we said. My worry was what they would say in public, in front of my family. I am not sure exactly what came over me, but I kept the course, walked ahead, and gave a genuine smile and a hello as we crossed paths.

I learned that after time had passed, we both needed the closure of that greeting to end that chapter in our lives so we could move forward to what was next. Here is the deal when you lead with empathy: you are not always going to be liked. With that said, it isn't acceptable to harbor resentment or bad feelings due to a past circumstance. Understanding others' perspectives and circumstances allows you to craft communication that best meets the situation. It doesn't mean you should worry about how they will respond or what they will say afterward behind your back.

School leaders don't need to be liked 100 percent of the time to lead. And honestly, if you were liked 100 percent of the time, are you really leading in the way that best supports your school?

Since that first situation, I have had many more like it. Sometimes staff members leave because they realize the fit isn't there anymore. Other times they recognize they want to try a different level or position. The toughest ones are the conversations and decisions that occur when everyone else sees the need for the person to leave in order to grow, but the person does not. In these situations, it seems there is no clear exit strategy, no way that we can both save face and feel like we made the right decision. People can say things that are truly hurtful. People can come at you in ways that they never would under normal circumstances and under less stress. These are the times when the valley seems deeper than usual, when there is no light to guide you, and when you feel the most isolated in the work you are called to do.

The moral of the story is this: don't get stuck in the mud. Be yourself, practice empathy for the other person in the situation, and move on rather than holding a grudge. School leaders don't need to be liked 100 percent of the time to lead. And honestly, if you were liked 100 percent of the time, are you really leading in the way that best supports your school? Giving feedback and making tough decisions are essential to ensuring we are all working toward a common vision and with the best supports and strategies at our fingertips. That doesn't mean we should do it in the harshest way possible. Leading with empathy allows us to make those decisions without becoming hard, harsh people. Instead, we must listen, be patient and open to what we are communicating, and remain open to what we are receiving as well.

LEAD**FORWARD**STRATEGY
Keep It Real

Leading with empathy and being open to what the other person is saying allows you to listen and learn in every setting and context. This requires that you stick to your authenticity and vulnerability, and continue practicing those soft skills to improve your relationships. It all starts with one simple truth: no matter the situation, be your empathetic self.

- **Be yourself.** You can be in a classroom, or at the grocery store in your sweatpants, no makeup, and three-day hair. It doesn't mean you get to change who you are or your attitude toward your staff or students. Don't question the decisions you've recently made, regardless of who you're facing. No matter your location or looks, be yourself. Say hi and ask how the recent assessment went or how an older sibling is doing.

- **Remember to be a person first, a title second.** When making tough decisions that impact personal relationships, that thick skin has to shed a few layers. Be sensitive to another after a difficult conversation, and don't start to isolate yourself or others. While these conversations are uncomfortable, walking away or avoiding the other person afterward means the message is lost. In short, you're making it personal rather than professional—and that's not empathy. Instead, amend the relationship however you can, and go out of your way to make sure the person knows that you've moved past the unpleasantness. You will improve your relationships and prove yourself as a leader, just by practicing those small, authentic kindnesses.

- **Avoid awkward silence at all costs.** The other person is probably just waiting for you to make the first move, and as the leader, it's part of your job. Practice empathy here too, and realize that you can't stand back and wait for them to come to you, no matter how much you might want to. If you're in a particularly difficult situation, a script might help here as well. Prepare several pieces of small talk, then seek the person out, smile, wave, and start a conversation with them.

Person, Principal, or Both?

The phone call came in late, but when I saw who was calling, I immediately picked up and started joking with the person on the other line like we normally did in our professional relationship. Immediately after my first one-liner, I knew something was wrong. Her response wasn't another funny joke but a statement that something incredibly hard had just happened in her family's life. That something was going to pull her away from work. She was a shell of who she was before for a long, long time afterward. And due to the circumstances and the community in which we lived, no one else knew for a long time. During those first few weeks, my professional role blurred with the personal. Late-night calls, weekend check-ins, and my authentic way of empathizing with semi-inappropriate cards continued for a while. We had code texts and visual cues for when things got too big, at which point I would play like I didn't know anything so she could get through the lesson, staff meeting, or parent conference. While I wish I could say this situation was a singular event, it is one example among many where people are going through a dark period in their lives, and I was there to help them.

I knew early on that I would never be the person who made the casserole when someone was going through a tough time. Instead, I would be the person who listened. The one who suggested a book to read, a blog to follow, or a therapist to talk to during the dark times. I could give gift cards for coffee shops, manicures, or pizza places. For a long time, I would feel bad that I couldn't offer what most other people did. But after we climbed out of the pit, I often found out that they were getting homemade meals from someone else, and what they also needed—and what they found in me—was an unbiased ear to listen to the yuck and not judge. They needed a leader who extended a period of grace that others would question and sometimes judge. They needed a leader who relentlessly bubble-wrapped them in times of struggle and crisis until they were able to get on their feet again.

Interacting with family members after a tough school situation can also make me want to hide in my house after work. In the early days of my career, a student's parent passed away halfway through the child's first year of school. This child was five and no longer had a mom to go home to every night. The community was saddened and shocked. I was new in the position and had yet to deal with this circumstance as a school leader. Unsure of what to say or do, I just showed up. I went to the funeral where I didn't speak the language that was being sung and spoken. I sat in a pew and attempted to participate as authentically as I could without having a full understanding of what was being said. And at the end of that event, I gave the student a hug.

Looking back, I could have done more. But what I did do I did with a level of care and empathy for that family and community.

Leading with empathy is not easy, and at times it can be downright heartbreaking. However, building soft skills such as listening, patience, and a willingness to seek understanding outside of your own perspective will build relationships that last. I've been through this a lot. I have been to funerals; I have been to court. I have sat with families when they are making the decision to have their child go into inpatient psychiatric care, and I have held the hands of parents when they are at the lowest and looking for help. These situations were never outlined in my coursework. I don't remember writing reflections in college on what to say from the perspective of a teacher or leader when terrible things happen to your children.

That doesn't make them or the empathy you're showing any less important, or any less necessary.

No one expects you to show up as your best self with all the answers all the time. What they need is someone who will listen and walk alongside them, or simply sit in the row toward the back of the church.

LEAD**FORWARD**STRATEGY
Show Up, Title Optional

Some of my best moments in leadership happened when I showed up for something without my title, nametag, or business card. Caring for those you serve sometimes means just showing up as yourself, listening, and staying still in their presence.

- **Listen.** What is really going on? Don't make assumptions from the narrative you hear from others. Ask questions to get the big picture of what has happened, and what the people impacted might need.

- **Learn.** We all experience grief differently. If you are
  spending time with a family during a difficult circumstance, don't assume that they experience loss in the same
  way you would. When you are entering into a situation of
  deep sadness for others, just show up without judgment.
  My dear friend and mentor knew right where to find
  me hours after we learned some devastating news. I had
  gone into work. While some might judge my decision to
  complete paperwork and finish emails during the deepest
  pit of my adult life, my friend knew that in that moment,
  I needed to move forward and not fall into a deep, dark
  depression. He sat with me, listened to me, and had no
  judgment about the way I was dealing with my grief (and
  state of denial). Nine years later, I can't quite remember
  what he said to me, but I do remember that he stayed
  with me through the darkness.

- **Care.** As you care for others in your school community,
  do not be afraid to demonstrate care in your own authentic
  way. Maybe it is sitting with the children while the family
  completes paperwork, attending a concert with a family
  who recently lost a mother or father, or making that hot
  dish for a teacher who is grieving a significant loss. As
  long as you show up authentically, the other person will
  see your care the way you mean for them to see it.

How Do You Look When You Lead?

I am conscious of what I wear when I head to school. Yes, some
days I have to dress in a certain way for a certain meeting, but most
days, I try to wear something that signifies to others that I am not
a principal in a black suit, but a person willing to learn and lead
together in this work. I am most conscious about what I wear when

I am completing interviews with first-year teachers, paraprofessionals, office administrative staff, and cafeteria employees. During these interview days, I refuse to wear formal suits and instead focus on the idea that what I wear shows that I am excited to meet them, and am a person just like they are.

Too often, the person I am interviewing feels anxious before they walk into the room. Their own doubts diminish their belief in their ability to be amazing in the work they were called to do, and they are shy and quiet in the interview. From that perspective, I have chosen to lead differently during these interviews. First, my interview team is small with only two to three people. I attempt to hold the interview in an office instead of in a large conference room, and I get rid of the panel style of interviewing. You know, the kind where the interviewee is on one side of the table and four people are sitting on the other side with clipboards. For teacher interviews, we send a few of the questions ahead of time so they can come in confident about a few answers and lead off with something they have prepared. Before the candidate walks into the interview, one of us gives them a tour and talks about what they will experience in the interview, as well as the timeline. I am a believer in giving people the deal up front. If you want to build a trusting, honest school culture full of empathy, you have to start with empathy—before the candidate even gets the job.

LEADFORWARDSTRATEGY
Show Empathy in the Hiring Process

Listening and empathy aren't always about the discussion. They also include setting up the space to make it comfortable for the other person to speak.

- **Optimize the physical space.** Review the location of the interview. What does the room say about the school? Are you seeking a candidate who is excited about learning and building relationships, and does your space reflect that? I have asked people to come in and sit in the room as if they were being interviewed, and then asked them for feedback on the experience based on room aesthetics. Small details can make a big impact on how people see you and the school, and how comfortable they are in the meeting itself.

- **Plan ahead for a smooth process.** How are you setting the stage for a successful experience for the candidate? Send questions ahead of time, including a link to a video introducing the school. Test any tech equipment in advance to ensure the Google Hangout, Skype, or Zoom session goes off without a glitch. Investing this effort on the front end ensures a successful interview for all parties, and allows everyone to feel part of a collaborative effort.

- **Remember the person behind the position.** When was the last time *you* went through an interview? Do you remember how you felt and what you were thinking before, during, and after? Practice empathy for others and take time as a team to discuss how to make this experience positive for all parties.

Go Ahead and Ugly Cry

As leaders, we must make tough decisions and difficult calls every day. Most days, the worst repercussion is a post on social media or a piercing glare as the other party leaves our office. But one week, I remember responding to a number of family calls after we sent letters in regard to failing grades. We were recommending summer school and possible retentions, and families were not happy. These calls were tough. It wasn't the first time the families had heard the message, but this was the first directive toward a final decision. One such call started really dark. The mom was yelling and crying hysterically, claiming that the teachers, the office, and I didn't do enough to support her and her child. She almost didn't make sense at some points, and she turned the call into an opportunity to scream about everything that had gone wrong in her life and how that was a result of what we did or didn't do that year for her child. The call ended abruptly when she hung up on me. I remember feeling stung, but I went on with the rest of my day.

When we listen well, we are offering a space for the other person to talk out the situation, strategize, and come up with solutions. We are sitting next to them, not solving it for them.

Two days later, she attempted to kill herself.

The police came to the school, as the attempt happened after the kids arrived at school that day, and the authorities were following their plan for the children to go elsewhere while their mom was hospitalized. I remember walking into the teacher's classroom to give the teacher an update, informing the school social worker, and making sure we operated as normal until the guardian could get into town and tell the kids herself. After I did what I was supposed to do, I went back into my office, got my purse and went to my car, drove three blocks away, and proceeded to ugly cry. I called my mentor and between deep breaths attempted to explain the situation. He assured me of what my head already knew, but my heart needed to hear: this was not my fault.

So often, when we lead with grace and empathy, we attempt to take the whole load for others, when they just need a little help or someone to walk alongside them on the journey. Leaders need to become better listeners and less-accomplished fixers. Building the soft skills of listening and openness doesn't include fixing problems for others. Most often, when we listen well, we are offering a space for the other person to talk out the situation, strategize, and come up with solutions. We are sitting next to them, not solving it for them. When we take on someone else's load, we lose sight of our own. The pressure of taking on other people's problems starts to seep into our own homes and interactions with others.

Watch for signs in those around you who may be fatigued from taking on other people's stress, sadness, and dark times. Taking on too much can cause secondary trauma and impact lives beyond that person's immediate circle. Tell those around you, and model for them, that self-care is not selfish, but lifesaving. Give permission to ugly cry and release the stress brought on by others, rather than taking it home.

LEADFORWARDSTRATEGY
Put on Your Oxygen Mask First

Listening and observing are soft skills that we tend to forget to use in times of crisis or emergency. Taking the time to slow down and survey the surroundings and those impacted by the circumstances will allow you to lead with more intention and greater care than if you had just delegated or done things right away.

- **Recognize the signs.** Are you more tired than normal? Feeling isolated, or like no one understands what you are going through? Whatever your triggers are in the rough seasons, identify them right away so you can seek support. You can't help others if you're not helping yourself. Utilizing empathy in your interactions is a delicate balance of learning to care for others without carrying everything for them.

- **Ask for help.** When you are in the deep end of a situation with another person or a struggling student, make sure you check in on your own health. Maybe it is a walk break in the day or keeping your phone with you because of possible urgent calls regarding a parent or child. Whatever you need to help you cope, please ask. The people who want to help won't know what to do unless you tell them what you need.

- **Seek professional guidance.** Sometimes our hearts are not big enough for the hurt. Seeking professional counselors or medical attention is a way for someone from the outside to offer a hand to help you get back on course. Taking the time to identify our own emotions alongside those of others allows us to have honest conversations about where we are and whether we need a little extra help as well.

We Try Too Hard, Care Too Much

Secondary trauma continues to be a more prevalent buzzword in education. While I am grateful for this heightened focus on self-care for educators, it is also important to note that this isn't a new phenomenon, but something educators have dealt with all along. Leading with grace means recognizing the fine line of when helping others actually starts to hurt yourself. Being a listener can come at a cost if we take what we are hearing back to our homes and allow it to impact the joy we seek in our personal relationships and passions.

When you learn that a student is experiencing things outside of school that seem unimaginable and heartbreaking, it's hard not to carry their baggage in your own backpack. Leading with empathy requires us to listen to those closest to us when we might be getting close to falling off the balance beam between caring enough and caring too much. I am terrible at hiding this at home. My husband knows when a day was bad based on my face when I walk in the door. I realize that sometimes I become over-reflective: What could I have done differently? How could I have protected them? What could I have done sooner? What will happen to them? Will their family show up angry at me? Will the student be mad at me?

As an administrator, we often hear more details about situations than teachers hear, and it can take a toll on our self-care. I remember feeling connected to a new student in our school. His school record looked more like a seasoned traveler's passport. Multiple schools, double-digit foster homes, and a record within many courts and police systems. Something in his eyes and his interactions told the bigger story, and I was relentless in trying to get that narrative to be the first thing people saw in him, instead of his file. We talked a lot, and worked through frustrating situations, and started to see progress in school. The narrative was slowly changing, and I could see that in his eyes and heart. One night, I saw him show up at an after-school event with students who no longer attended our school, and tried to quietly check in to see if he needed an out, a way to keep himself out of trouble. But before I could get him to stay with me, he left with them.

And then he was labeled a runaway. The next day, I did my hallway supervisions, classroom observations, and meetings, and I checked email and called law enforcement to see if he had been found. The following day, I did the same. That night, I saw a book we had been talking about reading on my table at home, and suddenly the tears just started. Why didn't I stop him from leaving that night? Why couldn't he see that those friends were not going to help him stay on this new path? Would he be found safe? And if so, would he ever talk to me again? It was a week later before I learned he had been located. In that time, my emotions would surface at unexpected times and in unexpected ways. Honestly, it was almost like I was responding as if he was my own child—and truthfully, how many of you feel the same way about some of your students?

When you care too much, you try too hard. All of a sudden, the boundaries between school and home are barely visible. The concerns and sadness from school won't leave your mind, even when you're at home. These are the times when I am most withdrawn from those who can help. When we are intentional with our efforts of using empathy, we realize that along with listening and openness, we need to be open with others about needing help ourselves.

Caring too much is like your heart is one hundred times bigger than your brain. You know logically that you did what you could, but your heart hurts in a way that makes it difficult to cope. Remember what I said in the last section, and what you've heard so often from others: you can't help others if you don't help yourself first. Leading with empathy means showing empathy to those in your care, and also yourself. Being open with your feelings and turning to others for support or tagging out of a situation are not signs of weakness, but signs of great strength. We can't pour our energy and joy out to others when our own cup is empty. Finding ways to replenish our own cup, and asking for help, are essential if we're going to build that empathy muscle.

LEAD**FORWARD**STRATEGY
Gently Play Your Heartstrings

Leading with empathy requires the essential soft skill of openness to each circumstance and our response to it. We must recognize the emotional and physical toll some of this work takes on our own personal and professional lives. Asking for help and modeling that it's okay to ask shows those around us that we're building a safe, trusting space where we all can feel the empathy we need.

- **Stop trying to steer the ship.** When working through a process with others, don't try to control the action, which will consume your energy and lead you off course in your own life. Be patient and just be present for the person you're attempting to help.

- **Reasonably check in.** Check in with others in difficult times, but don't consume yourself with a high frequency. While extending care to others is essential in this work, you can't care to a point where you're damaging your own health. If you feel yourself becoming all-consumed by one situation at the risk of ignoring yourself or others, seek support and take breaks.

- **Lift others up in the work.** One thing I have learned during hard times is to pay the positive forward. After a rough day, I force myself to send out positive thank-you notes to staff, students, or members of my PLN. These acts of gratitude are meaningful to the receivers and help shift my thoughts toward those who raise me up rather than those who tear me down.

Thought Bubbles Not Talk Bubbles

The secret to growing as a leader is keeping that fire in your belly, and not letting it come out of your mouth. Not everyone wants your opinion all the time. And sometimes, your idea isn't nice or needed in the current conversation. In circumstances where one or both of the communication parties are frustrated, upset, or stressed, an added opinion or comment could escalate a situation quickly.

In these moments, I revert to my days as an autism teacher and the use of social stories or cartoons. When our students struggled to understand a social situation or misstep, we would cartoon the characters in action and put thought bubbles above their heads and talk bubbles as a triangle attached to a cloud. These two symbols signified two different actions: what we think and what we say.

We often misuse or swap out talk bubbles and thought bubbles in our daily conversations. When we are tired, frustrated, or upset, the filter between the two might get lost, and we say hurtful things. Sometimes these things are hard to repair or take back. Recognizing when you're about to insert a thought instead of stopping the comment is essential to maintaining relationships. What are your triggers? Are you more likely to slip up when you are tired, when you have too many things going on, or when you are late to another meeting and want to get something off your plate? Checking in with your triggers will prevent you from saying something you can't take back, and will help you keep friendships and relationships.

Finding strategies to keep you from slipping up is also critical in communication work. At the moment before you speak, write it down. Looking at words before they come out of your mouth gives you a filter to see whether those statements will help, hurt, or harm the conversation. Asking for a moment to think before you respond is also a great strategy. I am a processor and can say that my quick responses to questions and requests are usually my worst decisions. Asking for time to think about an issue isn't a sign of weakness; it is a signal to another person that their question is so essential that you need time to think about it. You want to give them a meaningful response, and it's hard for someone to get angry about that.

LEAD**FORWARD**STRATEGY
Cool Your Jets

Just as there are many ways to respond to a comment or conversation, there are many strategies to keep you from saying something. My go-to is the thought bubble/talk bubble, but you need to find the one that works for you. The following pointers will give you a start.

- **Take a pause.** An immediate reaction doesn't mean a quick response. Permit yourself time to process. If you need to, tell the other person that you need a moment to think about your answer. In the end, it will help everyone come to the best decision.

- **Game face on.** When a strange request or an out-of-the-box question or comment gets thrown your way, keep your poker face on so your words and expression match. If you give a verbal response that doesn't match your expression, it will confuse everyone and lead to problems down the line.

- **Come into it focused, not frustrated.** Check in with your body and stress level. If your emotions are high due to a schedule delay, a parent call, or a circumstance not tied to this interaction, ask for a moment or see whether the conversation can be delayed until you are in the right frame of mine.

MOVING**FORWARD**

Someone who leads with empathy can also be seen as a servant-minded leader. Taking into consideration others' feelings and working to find ways to serve and help them are essential when it comes to leading schools to higher achievement and deeper relationships. How often do you walk the halls of the school and ask, "How are you today?" How often do you take the time to listen to the answer and the undertones in the response? School becomes family, and we get good at reading each other. Who is off today? Did a family pet just pass away, did the divorce finalize last week, is it the anniversary of the death of a parent? Whatever the circumstance, the more time we take to check in with each other, the less isolated everyone feels. These check-ins are equally important to our own mental, emotional, and physical well-being.

Every year, I am supposed to go to the doctor for my annual checkup. You know the one: weight, height, blood test, blood pressure check, a few questions, and off you go. Now, if I don't remember to make the appointment, I miss it … maybe a few years in a row. In education, those checkups could parallel the evaluation process. Either once a year or maybe even every three years, we sit down, look in-depth at learning targets and goals, and discuss growth.

I challenge you not just to schedule checkups with your staff, but check-ins as well. Instead of focusing on the formal, scheduled, and prescribed meetings, add in informal, personal check-ins. How much do you know about the staff you serve alongside? How many children do they have, what did they dream of being when they grew up, and what did they do over spring break? Spending more unscheduled and natural check-in time allows you to look for symptoms of stress and burnout, as well as any other indications of a change in their ability to love what they do. Leading with empathy includes releasing judgment toward others and focusing on building each other up instead of tearing each other down.

CHAPTER 3
LEADFORWARDJOURNAL

Get grounded with your community

Building empathy requires me to create background knowledge about the individuals I serve. I will walk the school and write down at least three personal things about each staff member whose room I walk by. I will try to use these facts in my next conversation with each person.

List ways that I can invest in others ...

_____

_____

_____

_____

_____

_____

_____

_____

_____

_____

_____

_____

_____

_____

_____

Share your journal entries and ideas at #LeadForward on Twitter.

Grace with Integrity

Be Who You Are No Matter Who Is Watching

Integrity is doing the right thing even when no one is watching.
— C.S. LEWIS, AUTHOR

Lace Up

LEADING WITH GRACE and integrity is hard work. A person of integrity doesn't do the work for awards and accolades; they do the work because they are dedicated to the mission. Grace with integrity means doing the hard work without expecting credit. A strong work ethic is assumed and not celebrated. No one will give you a sticker for coming to work every day on time—but some people expect it. A person with integrity is focused and manages time and tasks well. They are the go-to person, and the one others always want for group work. The ones who get things done. This skill is ingrained in one's actions and built over time.

When I think of integrity, I think of a marathon. Training for a marathon takes months, sometimes years. I get up, lace up, and go out for more runs than most people realize that it takes to train for 26.2 miles. My lifestyle changes; I go to bed earlier so I can get in three extra miles the next morning before work; I start to watch what I eat, and I drink water all the time. Here is the interesting thing about marathons: in the end, it isn't about how long it took me to run 26.2 miles; it is about the twenty-six weeks of training I accomplished to get to that day. And then guess what? Usually a few days after a big race, I get up and start training all over again.

> *Educators are the bravest people I know. You get up, show up, and demonstrate such character in the face of adversity from all angles.*

Leading with integrity is a daily task, and one that most won't recognize or see. I have seen leaders who say they have integrity, but can't consistently show up and display it. They start the year with agendas and a detailed site plan, but fast forward three months and the agendas are done—and sometimes the meetings are as well. Educators put their lives into their work, and need leaders who show the same ethics in their work practice. Graceful leaders with integrity show up every day, even when they aren't feeling their best, because they know that someone needs them. They are resilient in not giving up, in trying a new teaching strategy to support a few students, in repairing a relationship with a student who was hurt by a consequence, and in saying hi to that family member who is frustrated with how their child is doing in school and feels like it is all the leader's fault.

In short, they are the people who do the hard work even when no one is watching.

Integrity in this work takes grit. On the days I didn't want to go out for a run, I still got up, laced up, and ran—even if it was only two miles instead of four. At school, I have had the "Starbucks" moment in which I doubted my gifts in this work and wondered if I would serve better as a Starbucks barista than a school teacher. Regardless of my inner doubts, I parked the car and walked in the door and back into the classroom. Educators are the bravest people I know. You get up, show up, and demonstrate such character in the face of adversity from all angles. Most of you don't even recognize how much integrity you show others because it is just in your nature. What you do in your classroom and your school is just what you do. No medal needed.

LEADFORWARDSTRATEGY
Create Your Own Training Plan

Are you ready to take your leadership with grace to the next level? The soft skill of integrity takes the most resiliency. Practicing a strong work ethic and becoming skilled at getting things done takes patience, persistence, and a strong plan.

- **What is your goal?** Dreaming big means taking small first steps. Building a leadership style with integrity starts with creating a big goal and then taking small, actionable steps. What is your daily intention? What do you want to try to do better today than yesterday? Setting short- and long-term goals keeps you focused on what you are setting out to do. Each day, write out a list of what you are grateful for and what you are looking forward to. Extend this to long-term goals and the baby steps it will take to get there. Writing these things down will keep you accountable and show you the path toward the finish line.

- **Train for it.** Trying to reach a specific student or looking to enhance your capabilities in certain communication skills? Do the research. When you're training for a race, you don't start with a ten-mile run. You lay the foundation first. Training for a goal is no different. Read articles, books, and blogs, and ask others how they started. Create a plan and start on Day One, not Day Twenty.

- **Pace yourself.** Leading with integrity can be emotionally and physically exhausting, and having a strong work ethic can be confused with working 24/7. If you're a great manager, you might find yourself taking over responsibilities that belong to others. But that's a symptom of controlling, not leading. When you start to take over instead of supporting, you will begin to see emotional and physical stress in your life. Just like runners who try to run a marathon their first time out, you're taking on too much. Recognize the signs that you might need to walk for a bit instead of run, and ask others to work with you on this journey. It makes it so much more enjoyable!

Don't Let It Go!

I have some pretty wild ideas. From Human Hungry, Hungry Hippo to completely throwing out our kindergarten assessment and starting from scratch. When I lead, I might do it in an unconventional way. Regardless, I always start with an idea, dream, or goal, and I don't let it go. Some people consider me to be stubborn in my work. I will sit, walk, and talk through the idea and ruminate on it for days. I will use Voxer, email, Google Hangouts, or coffee meetings to ask others how they have done similar work. I will read book upon book and find recent research articles that talk about the project, and it tends to consume my mind and conversation. Once a plan is in place, I start to use the process of empathy mapping to see if I have thought of the other angles and people this work will impact.

My perseverance can quickly turn into an all-consuming passion for whatever project I am working on at the time. While on the outside, this ability to persevere can be a blessing or a curse, I like to look at it as plain old persistence. I just don't quit. I might have to take a pause in the plan or change course a bit to get to the final destination, but I rarely let a good idea get away.

A recent example of this was finding a way to increase the number of students who passed courses at our middle school. We started by reviewing last year's data: which students had the hardest time passing classes, and why? During weekly meetings, we measured and monitored the amount of missing work students had accumulated and created "mid-quarter" catch days as a way to pause on new material and catch up, retake, or turn in assessments and assignments. Our end-of-quarter celebrations switched from celebrating behavioral success to celebrating academic goals. Only students who were passing all classes could participate, and we let them know weeks in advance.

Slowly, our data started changing. We noticed that by paying attention to specific students, monitoring missing work on a weekly basis, and celebrating students for growth gains, our data changed. The number of students with F's on their report cards started to drop—while school attendance rose. And at these academic cele-brations, students were proud of not only the character they demon-strated every day, but also the grades they were starting to receive.

Looking back at many points on the journey, you could have con-sidered this work a failure. There wasn't a significant change between the first and second quarters. It took more time and new reporting tools to get teachers the missing work reports they gave students, and there was pushback on "rewarding" students for turning in work that was already required. In the end, we learned a lot and built a foundation to start from when we run this program again next year—a foundation we wouldn't have had if we had stopped at the first roadblock. Instead, we let our integrity take the wheel and worked through the problems, knowing that we were on the right track—and that we were doing the right thing for our students.

When have you had an idea and had others tell you to stop? Or worse, tell you not to even start? Leading with integrity requires you to look away from the people in the crowd who disagree with your decision or the direction you are taking to the destination, and listen to your gut instead. Don't let someone else's lack of vision derail your integrity or authenticity.

LEADFORWARDSTRATEGY
Stay Dedicated to the Dream

People, the work is hard, but it is worth it. Stay focused on what you and your team have set forth as goals for the year, and stop taking on just ... one ... more thing. Leading with grace and integrity and utilizing soft skills such as focus and confidence means you stay clear and tight with the right work, and say no to anything that blocks your way.

- **Find your why.** What is the overarching reason you do what you do? Figure that out and hold onto it. Keep it in front of you. That is your motivation for reaching the goals you set. For details and examples of how to find your why, see the first book in the Lead Forward Series, *Be Excellent on Purpose* by Sanée Bell.

- **Stay grounded in the what.** Be cautious and don't let other people's ideas pull you away from your original intention. Build your plan for achieving your goal, include your "why" to give you the motivation, and then stick to it. While it is completely okay to take a step back and come at the idea from another direction, make sure that step back doesn't move you away from what you started out to accomplish in the first place.

- **Celebrate your who.** Mini-celebrations are required in this work. Make those mini-celebrations about the "who" behind your "why," and make them part of your team. Data retreats, student celebrations, and shout-outs to families—with data included—are little ways to celebrate the journey toward the big prize at the end.

Lean Into the Fear

Leadership is lonely. I wish I could sugarcoat this, but I can't. As a leader, you are responsible for many people and decisions. Much of your work is done behind the scenes and those you serve only get part of your perspective. Sometimes the decisions are met with smiles and high-fives. Other times the decisions you make are met with tears, anger, and even posts on social media. In the dark times when you feel like you are never going to get out of the pit, it is easy to let shame and denial cover up all of the good around you.

I love the visual of seasons in this work. Currently, I am in the winter. Things are cold and dark. I keep searching for sunshine, and I'm met with snow days and temps that are well below zero. I haven't seen sunshine in a long time, so it's easy to think I won't see it again. But logically, I know that is not true. Spring will come again, the grass will turn green, flowers will bloom, and the decisions that were tough to make will eventually turn into something beautiful.

Leaning into the fear of stepping out, or making a decision you know will lead to an unfavorable response, is scary. Even seasoned leaders can feel paralyzed in these situations. For a split second, or for weeks, you might teeter between doing what is right and doing what is easy. Leading with grace and vulnerability means that it is okay to admit this. Tell a close friend or a mentor what you are struggling with right now. Paint the picture and ask for help on how to get where you want to go. Recently, I reached out to multiple mentors and asked them to help me deliver a difficult message. I literally practiced it multiple times and asked for honest feedback. *Here is what I am trying to say. Did that come across?* And sometimes when I am walking into the discussion, I let the other person know that this will be hard.

It is okay to share your fear and doubt when leading. Starting out that way in the conversation shows the other party that your guard is down, the weapons of words are off the table, and you are ready to engage in work that is meaningful and productive. You are inviting them to join you at that table. Letting your perfection guard down and stripping your titles, your awards, and your accomplishments from the conversation levels the playing field and opens the door for an interaction that might lead to future relationships that benefit everyone.

LEADFORWARDSTRATEGY
Create a Template for Tough Conversations

Having these tough conversations isn't easy, but it is necessary. They don't get easier the more you have them, and they shouldn't. When you are leading with vulnerability, each conversation requires sincerity and a genuine response to the other party. Finding a way to meet in the middle and go from there allows you both to find a common starting ground. Regardless of what you say, how you practice, or what happens next, the most important step is to start the conversation.

- **Be direct.** Practice what you are going to say ahead of time to make sure you come across the way you want to. Write it down. Tough conversations can be nerve-wracking, so practice being clear, direct, and concise. Setting the stage for the conversation also gives the other person a chance to prepare. You might schedule a time to talk, and within the subject line state your purpose. The memo might read like this: *While I know you and your true intentions, we need to talk about a recent email and how your words impacted the receiver of your message.* Being specific and direct lets the other person know that you are entering into a conversation to seek more information and to find a solution to the problem.

- **Be sensitive.** When you are on the receiving end of a tough conversation, pay attention to what the other person has to say. As hard as it is for you to respond, it was harder for the other person to come to you in the first place. Recognize the other person's effort in sending the message and allow your guard to come down and your gloves to come off. When you have to start a conversation, lead with your heart and you will set a positive tone. For example: *I know you and that your heart is in this work, and this will be a tough conversation. However, in order for us to get better in the work, we need to walk through what happened yesterday so we can put plans in place to keep it from happening again.*

- **Be solution-driven.** What is the outcome you hope for with this conversation? Be specific with yourself. For example, it might be to clearly convey to the other person that no matter how frustrated they are in the moment, the action they took at that time can never happen again. It could be trying to read between the lines of side comments in meetings and combating past practices of not being engaged in staff meetings.

Whatever the situation, try to focus on an end outcome that is acceptable to all, while identifying what everyone needs to move forward. For example: *I sense that you have been hurt by the school system, and that hurt comes across in your written communication to our staff. I don't know how to fix your past disappointments but I want to meet and discuss how we can move forward.*

Not an Invitation for Your Opinion

Too often, I have accidentally opened a door or my mouth, or posted a message or tweet as an invitation for others to critique or criticize something I have done or wanted to do.

That is on me, not on them.

Other people's opinions are just that. Their opinions don't matter more than your core beliefs do. Their opinions shouldn't stop you from starting something you know is right. What they say, tweet, post, or do at and toward you should never prevent you from trying something. Other people don't fully understand or see your vision. They do not walk in the classrooms you walk in every day, have connections with the families you serve, or appreciate the staff you work with the way you do. They certainly do not have the authentic grace and service you apply in your day-to-day interactions. However, we too often put these strangers' opinions on a pedestal and turn away from what we know we should do based upon our interactions with them.

I worry about educators when they're engaging on social media. I see people post something they wanted to share and celebrate, only to see others shame and discredit their ideas. I worry that the one negative post or comment will stop many ideas and dreams from being created and shared with the rest of us. I am sad to think of the ideas and dreams we haven't gotten to see because people are too afraid to try again.

Just because someone offers you feedback doesn't mean you need to do anything with it. Learn how to handle feedback in a gracious manner and you will make the other person feel as if they have been heard, while deciding for yourself whether the feedback is helpful.

When I said at the beginning of this section that it is on me, I meant it. Even yesterday, someone made a comment about something I said on social media and I immediately retreated and wanted to respond. My feelings of doubt quickly snuck up on me. Remember that while someone out in the world might say something about you, it doesn't mean you have to respond. If you didn't ask for that opinion, blow it off. Your integrity and vision are the important skills here, and nothing should get in the way of you following them.

Leading with grace and integrity means knowing how to stick to your guns no matter what anyone else does or says about your ideas and dreams. It's about how you react to them, not about them being allowed to react to you. Be careful not to listen to the critics or commentary from the cheap seats. Share your ideas and listen to the cheers. Silence the jeers. Learn to do that and you will keep your ability to lead the work forward in a positive light.

LEAD**FORWARD**STRATEGY
Thanks, but No Thanks

Just because someone offers you feedback doesn't mean you need to do anything with it. Learn how to handle feedback in a gracious manner and you will make the other person feel as if they have been heard, while deciding for yourself whether the feedback is helpful, hurtful, or unnecessary in your decision-making.

- **Don't engage.** Not everything needs a response. If someone retweets or comments on your post and takes away from your intentions, don't reply. If a parent is pushing you into a corner in regard to a colleague or a staff member you supervise, and is looking for you to agree or say something negative, stay silent. Engagement equals agreement and can pull you into something you don't have time for and need to stay away from.

- **Delete from your brain.** Keeping up with the comments from others that detract from your work keeps your brain full of static and puts a roadblock in your way. If someone says something and it is shaming or hurtful, don't allow those words to seep into the actions and integrity you show to others. In the moment, put your phone down or step away from the computer and get some fresh air. Letting the negative go allows you time to build up the positive and productive comments and thoughts you need for the work to come.

- **Model the way.** The best way to ignore the haters and negative noise is to post the positive. Take time to remark on someone else's work in a positive and productive light. For every negative comment you receive, turn around and give five positive and productive remarks to others. This habit will help you recognize who is important and why you do the work you do, and show others how we can lift each other up in this world that resorts to cutting down.

Putting It in Reverse

In this work, there may be more mistakes than opportunities to move forward. When we're thinking of soft skills, the word *soft* comes to mind. Soft to me means delicate, fragile, and tender. Building these skills takes time, effort, and a lot of mistakes. Moving forward after a mishap with an interaction might mean we have to take a few steps back. I experience this often when building and rebuilding relationships with middle school students. Kindergartners are quick to forgive and forget. Seriously, we could have a sad conversation, and two minutes later I am getting hugs and high-fives. Middle school students, however ... their hurt takes longer to heal and requires authentic apologies and being vulnerable with them about mistakes.

Early on, and way too often, I assumed that if I apologized, we would be okay, and I attempted to just go back to the way it was. I didn't think about how much my words or missteps could impact a tween or teen, and wondered why our relationships never really felt the same. That was until I started working with Kenny. Kenny had a tough exterior and made sure every adult knew it. Through his special education programming and supports, he had additional help throughout the day, but was still navigating how to respond to adults and their requests. His responses were inconsistent at best. He could be my best friend one day and give me the stink eye the next, usually without warning or any interaction on my part. But on that Friday, I knew he would be mad, and I would deserve it.

I was going to have to let Kenny know he wouldn't be attending the dance that night due to some of his interactions earlier in the day. His teachers asked if I could wait until later in the day, as he had been looking forward to this event for a month and his classroom behavior had improved because of it. In the end, the interaction was brief, but my entry was tough. "Kenny, you are going to be disappointed in what I am going to say, and I am sorry." After I told him, he was angry and let me know that he felt my decision was unfair. He handled the news better than I expected, but refused to look my way for weeks.

I don't like to be told no, so having a student angry at me is difficult. I spent hours trying to figure out my entry point into a conversation to repair the damage that had been done. Finally, I just counted to five, no script prepared, and walked into the room.

Me: Kenny?

Kenny: What?

Me: Kenny, I know you are angry at me and I would like to have the opportunity to repair the relationship.

Kenny: I don't care anymore.

Me: Okay, well here it is. I would like to buy you lunch, not from the lunchroom, but from an actual restaurant. I'd like to eat together and discuss how I might repair our relationship, as I would still like to be a person in your corner. Please let your teacher know when you might be willing to have lunch with me. I will wait as long as you need." I turned and started to walk out of the room.

Kenny: Well, I am free tomorrow.

Over McDonald's french fries and a chicken sandwich, Kenny and I repaired our relationship. Taking the time to take a few steps back moved our relationship in a direction we wouldn't have gone in if that situation hadn't happened.

Lesson learned: mistakes can make a relationship better if you are willing to admit that the mistake was made and work to repair it. Leading with integrity only works when you are willing to recognize that all stakeholders deserve an apology when you screw up. Further, everyone deserves the chance to give you feedback in terms of how your words and actions impacted them and what could go better next time. Asking for this type of feedback and practicing what you learn also shows your most vulnerable students that they matter, that someone cares about them, and that they have a voice. This takes courage, but it is always the right thing to do.

LEAD**FORWARD**STRATEGY
Fixing What You Broke

Leading with a strong work ethic requires that you know when you are doing the right thing, and how to fix it when that right thing goes wrong. It shows others that you may not be perfect, but you are willing to work on fixing your mistakes so you can be better next time.

- **Own it.** It is hard to fix something you don't think is broken. Repairing a relationship takes an honest apology, not one that includes a "but." Set aside time to make sure the other person is in a place to hear the apology. You might be ready to say you are sorry, but that doesn't mean the other person is ready to hear it. Read the room, watch the other party's body language, and from there decide whether it is the right time. If it's not, own the responsibility to come back another time when you might be able to apologize to a more open mind.

- **Find a way to repair it.** It might be lunch, a hand-written card, or an opportunity to have coffee with the other person. Use soft skills like the ability to be honest, problem-solving, and listening to find an authentic way to apologize to the other party. Show your integrity by sticking with it until you find the right way to repair the relationship.

- **Move forward.** After it is said and done, it is done. Making mistakes and owning them is important. Moving past them is essential. Move forward and don't rehash the mistake. Leading with integrity requires you to let go of past failures, as those thoughts will only weigh you down in your mind and decrease your confidence as you continue to lead with conviction and positive intentions.

The Meeting Before, During, or After the Meeting

Don't deny it; we have all been a part of pre- or post-meeting meetings. It could have been a staff meeting, a parent conference, an administrative team meeting, or a student assistance team debrief. You meet formally and have discussions, debates, and dialogues. Everyone leaves with tasks and accomplishments. Usually, a small group meets afterward and further discusses what occurred. There may be comments about what should have been said, some productive, some not. When it becomes toxic, the comments become personal, and sabotaging statements follow. And all of a sudden, what was said in the full meeting starts to dissolve based on the few people who continue the conversation after the meeting.

Sometimes, the meeting after the meeting comes before the meeting. Staff members' hidden agendas are prominent before the conversation even starts. Usually, the agenda comes out like "Everyone thinks this" or "We have always done that." Using group speak when it comes from one individual gives the statement more power. The best way to directly respond to these tactics is to ask for the group that's complaining to meet, or to call out the elephant in the next related meeting. If no one says anything when you ask, either it wasn't an issue to start with, or people have recognized that the point is not productive.

I have seen and been a part of this very thing during student support meetings. When we are supposed to be talking about a student, we end up talking about their great uncle, mother, or older siblings, who we have already served. We judge the student and their performance based on genetics rather than on themselves. That can't happen if you want to make real change. The moral of the story doesn't need to be written by the team and past family experiences, but by the student. Be careful to keep the one you're talking about front and center in your communication or you'll find yourself going off track.

Leading with grace and leaning into your communication soft skills in these situations requires clarity and focus in your conversations and agendas. Are we here to talk about the second cousin or the student sitting in front of us? Are we talking about what this meeting is addressing, or a problem that someone wants to blow out of proportion? It is vital to stay on point and stick to the meeting norms. If you don't have meeting norms, create them. Find a timekeeper to help you stay accountable to the time allotted to maintain a conversation focus, and use agendas to control the meeting narratives.

LEAD**FORWARD**STRATEGY
Revise Meetings to be Meaningful

Communication graces require vigilant work on clarity and focus when it comes to meetings. If you are attempting to change the pattern of behavior of a firmly established meeting, you must find a way to create new rules and stick to them. It is too easy to slip back into old, comfortable practices and end up with less productivity and more frustration. Using the following steps will help you move toward a more focused meeting template, which will provide better results in the end.

- **Find norms.** When I noticed we were getting more caught up in the family tree than the student we were currently serving, we set group norms about what we would discuss. If you have ever been to a Professional Learning Conference (PLC) Institute, you know that the DuFours have great examples of norms. Find a few best practices, share them with the team, and in the next meeting, dedicate fifteen minutes to creating your own team norms specific to the people at the table. What is the rule on cell phones? Sidebars? Comments and conversations not relevant to the task at hand? By stating the problems you have seen in previous meetings, you tackle the elephant in the room and communicate the high expectations you have for the team you are serving.

- **Set times.** Allow time in the meeting to debate and discuss concerning items and you will decrease those meetings after the meetings. Just make sure there is a start and stop time on these debates, so they don't monopolize the meeting.

- **Limit time spent on the data.** While ethical decision-making requires reliable data, be careful not to be inundated by numbers. When you focus too much on a current eighth-grader's third grade scores, you lose perspective of who the student is *now*. Make sure your meeting schedule keeps your team moving forward, rather than looking at old information.

- **Watch out for friendly advice.** While it is essential to have "safe" people who will listen to you vent and provide support, watch out for those who are trying to sway the work of the group through their connection to you. Remember, stick to the agenda and your goals for the meeting!

MOVING**FORWARD**

Integrity in our work is what we do when no one is watching, or when we are in our darkest hours. Leading with grace and integrity allows us to continue to find light in the darkest of places and shows others that no matter who is or isn't watching, we are the same person.

Ask your closest friends what words describe you. Perhaps some of these will sound familiar: dependable, reliable, good listener, caring, persistent, resilient, strong in character, servant leader … If you hit the mark on a few of those, you already utilize integrity in your personal life. Transitioning these skills into your professional life means taking your life's mission and making it part of your professional mantra. If your personal goals include ensuring that every student leaves the classroom or school knowing someone cared about them, then lead every day with a kind heart and make sure that you have meaningful and intentional conversations with others on a daily basis. If your passion is to ensure that all students have access to viable and rigorous coursework, then lead the work on your feet, spend time in classrooms, work with teachers in PLCs, and share data early and often with students, staff, the central office, and parents.

Reflect back on your biggest learning experiences. Did you learn because of the obstacles? Or in *spite* of them because of the drive, discipline, and relentless pursuit of what you wanted? Our training in integrity has brought us to the position we are in now, and it will lead us to continue to impact and influence others in whatever we choose to accomplish. Leading forward means you continue to do what is right, in both darkness and light.

CHAPTER 4
LEADFORWARDJOURNAL

Prep, prepare, and train

What one thing will I commit to trying every day?

_____

_____

_____

Who will hold me accountable for this new practice?

_____

_____

_____

How will I know I am intentional with this action?

_____

_____

_____

Focused, goal-oriented celebrations

What have I been working on for a while in school that I haven't taken the time to celebrate?

_____

_____

_____

How do I celebrate the success, big and small, with my staff as a team and individually?

_____

_____

_____

Abort, abort, abort!

Moving forward requires me to let go of the past. What is the one conversation or comment someone has said recently that I am still holding onto? Write it down, rip it up, and let it go.

_____

_____

_____

_____

_____

_____

_____

_____

_____

_____

_____

_____

Share your journal entries and ideas at #LeadForward on Twitter.

Communication Graces
Watch What You Say and How You Say It

The culture of any organization is shaped by the
worst behavior the leader is willing to tolerate.
— STEVE GRUENERT AND TODD WHITAKER,
AUTHORS OF *SCHOOL CULTURE REWIRED*

ALKING, TEXTING, TWEETING, Snapchatting, YouTubing, FaceTiming . . . you get the picture. The ways in which we communicate today have grown significantly. Each platform has its own social graces on how to communicate, and often, grammar and punctuation are not even required. While the mechanics are left up in the air, the message can be lost in translation if you break a hidden rule, you haven't fully focused on what you are saying or how you are saying it, or you aren't using the right platform. In this chapter, we will take a look at the meaning of our messages and the intended and unintended impacts and outcomes of our words—as well as the social graces we can use to protect ourselves.

What You Focus on Grows

Has this happened to you? You get an idea in your head and the more you focus on it, the more you find that you become aware of similar ideas or strategies faster and more frequently. It reminds me of when my husband was looking for a new car and he drove a specific model, and all of a sudden, I saw more of that model on the road. I recently found out that this is called the Baader-Meinhof effect, otherwise known as the frequency illusion. This effect, however, doesn't just come into play with cars and educational strategies; it can also appear with our thoughts and words.

Let's unfold this in our classrooms. Have you noticed that your focus can shift from appreciating the 95 percent of students doing what they need to do each day to obsessively awfulizing the 5 percent that don't seem to get it? And when we awfulize the 5 percent, it starts to consume 100 percent of our mind and time, and then the black hole of desperation and frustration sets in for all involved.

Now let's move this a little closer to our hearts, and sometimes our flaws. What about that one parent, that one teacher, or that one coworker that consumes too much of your time? Maybe they are always late to a meeting or they never seem to pull their weight in the work that needs to be accomplished. They might be a chronic complainer or have a habit that annoys you. No matter how egregious their fault may be (big or super small), we tend to exaggerate the time their lack of responsibility takes up for us.

When you create a daily habit of looking for the good and articulating it to others, your outlook will change and it will shape a culture of positive interactions and affirmations.

Now, this gets toxic when our thoughts become our words. Think about it. You have had enough of a coworker and a minor behavior that you have amped up to be a major one in your mind. Another staff member, a friend, or even your spouse asks the loaded question: "How is it going?" and you unload. Sometimes I wish I could see a written transcript of what I am about to say so I could pause or rewrite it before it came out. Maybe I would see how silly or blown out of proportion it was about to be. But we haven't invented that app yet. So instead, we spew out words that we can't take back, and make a situation or relationship with a colleague worse than it was before.

Instead of focusing on the 5 percent, start looking at the 95 percent. Send a note or make a call home to the student who consistently shows up ready to learn and sometimes feels like they aren't seen in your school. Take intentional time to interact with staff and students. Communication graces are built into each interaction and can enhance and build trusting relationships one talk, note, or text at a time—but only if you use them. When you create a daily habit of looking for the good and articulating it to others, your outlook will change and it will shape a culture of positive interactions and affirmations.

Ask questions and remember the answers. Check in on the staff member whose dog was sick last week, follow up with the student who is in transition between two homes after a recent divorce, and congratulate the members of the robotics team for the award at the state competition. Make more intentional time to focus on what is going well, and what is going wrong will start to fade into the background.

LEAD**FORWARD**STRATEGY
Sharpen Your Sights

If you want to build your skills of seeing and stating the good, start small, stay consistent, and build a habit of looking for the great things going on every day and talking about them. Focusing more on others and less on yourself enhances soft skills such as observation, listening, caring, and being intentional with your actions. People will notice that you are focusing on others rather than on yourself, and your relationships and ability to lead will grow.

- **Look for the good.** Keep a stack of notecards on your desk. Set a goal to write one to a staff member or student each week with a positive thought, feedback, or observation.

- **See something, say something.** When you see a student or staff member doing something that aligns with the work of the school, go up and say something. Pass positive affirmations forward and recognize others for things and you will move the culture of the school in the right direction.

- **Look inside before looking outside.** Feeling agitated for no known reason? Noticing that you are a little shorter in your responses to others than you usually are? If you can't remember the last time you took the time to recognize the good in someone else, you might have found the reason you are struggling with unknown aggression. Find the positive in life, and share it. You'll be rewarded with more balance inside yourself, and better relationships with those around you.

Leaving the Lounge

Early in my educational career, someone warned me of the place called the staff lounge. Walking into it, you would think it was a welcoming environment for adults to rest, recuperate, and build relationships with each other in twenty minutes or less. Most lounges have beautiful things on the bulletin board, a place to store and warm up your food, and sometimes even lovely chairs and tables. Inspirational quotes and sign-ups for social events fill the walls, books line the shelves, and at certain times of the year, you can even buy Girl Scout Cookies and other goods from fundraisers. I often thought an alarm would activate the moment a student tried to walk into this secret haven for staff in their brief break from teaching. Staff members put a lot of energy into making this place a warm and inviting room for all. At the beginning of the year, you could walk into the room and be greeted with smiles and gestures welcoming you to the table. Laughter and stories about what just happened in the classroom or over the weekend filled the air, and you could walk away after twenty minutes feeling ready to tackle the rest of the day.

And then it happens. At some point in the year, the environment and mood changes. The things on the walls stay up, but the feeling when you walk in is different. Sometimes you can sense it from one table: a lack of eye contact or the death glare to anyone who walks in. People clump up, and there seems to be less room at the table for you now than before. Conversations turn from lighthearted and funny to dark and depressing. You leave the lounge ready to leave the school, not prepared to go back to your room! What changed? And can we go back to the way it was?

When I was a new teacher (denim jumpers, apple pins, and all), I was an idealist. I loved learning and sharing stories, and looked forward to each day and the challenges it would bring. I would go in the lounge looking for connections with others and excited about building friendships, as I had moved far from home, friends, and family to take this position. I had high hopes that I could develop my PLN from a professional and personal lens, and looked forward to making friends in the building where I spent the majority of my waking hours. And while decades later, I still stay connected with people I met during my first years of teaching, I most remember the people who intentionally made it tougher. These were the ones who seemed to have hardened hearts. No matter what ideas I tried to offer, they responded with statements like, "That will never work," "I have tried that," or worse yet, "You haven't done this long enough to offer advice."

Ouch.

At a table in the lounge, the hardest part of these conversations was how one person could spin a topic negatively and see everyone else at the table give it momentum. All of a sudden, a student refusing to write in class turned into a more significant issue than it needed to be, and we left more frustrated with the student than we were when we walked into the staff lounge.

I noticed that I started to leave the lounge sad, angry, and frustrated for no reason. Most times, the students (or staff) who were discussed didn't have anything to do with me, but the truth is, I still participated. I wanted to belong, I wanted to contribute, and I wanted to start making friends in this new place. So I began to add my two cents when I had no business doing so. I found that at specific tables, the agreement came when my comments were more negative than positive, and while I enjoyed the sense of belonging at the moment, I felt worse when I left. And then, usually after a significant misstep or a moment when I realized that the gossiping was doing no good for myself or others, I left the lounge.

Reflecting on this situation now, I realize that I needed to be clearer in my mind about what I wanted. I was looking for a place to visit, reconnect, and plug into others. A space where I could go with problems and find solutions. I didn't want conversations that admired the problem or became negative and unproductive. Had I clearly articulated my concerns about the conversations and set some ground rules, I might have shifted those conversations in a more positive and productive direction. I might have shared with others what I was struggling with and what I needed.

Instead, I just stopped going to the lounge and started eating lunch in my classroom or with students. For a while, I felt like I was the only adult in a school full of teachers, and some days, the only people I talked to were my students. But then a change happened. Another teacher or two asked to eat in my classroom, or for me to eat in their room. My intentional action of leaving the lounge was seen by others as me seeking a different conversation for our thirty minutes away from our students. When it got nice out, we decided to eat our lunch and walk around the school, and on special occasions, we dashed to our cars and ran out to get something.

While I hated the pit and isolation I felt forced into when I walked away from the lounge, I learned that I loved finding a circle of other teachers who craved optimism, hope, and joy. We found our own space to cultivate that culture. And had I still been at that school when I felt confident in this skill, I would have gone back to that lounge and created a table that invited others who had similar beliefs and who were ready to walk away from the dark conversations for a little more light in their lives.

LEADFORWARDSTRATEGY
Where Do You Eat Your Lunch?

Do you currently have a space or place in your life like the lunch table? When we get sucked into groupthink and talk that is negative and unproductive, leading with grace in your communication requires you to state what you need and create what you want. If you're looking to build a place where you are lifting up others instead of cutting them down, you need to start by telling others what you are looking for. Chances are, others are trying to find it as well.

- **Inspect the environment.** Leading with soft skills requires the use of a different muscle, and can be impossible if you are stuck in a toxic environment or daily negative talk. What you do, what you discuss, and how you feel in those interactions in the lounge and the copy room impact how you teach and lead when you go back into the classroom and office. If the place in which you were spending your time is no longer serving these needs, then it is time to leave. Take a look around. Is there more negativity than positivity? Are there people who revel in the negative and spend too much time criticizing? Does spending time in that space make you feel exhausted? If so, it's time to move on.

- **Find your circle.** Who do you look up to in your school? Who is that one person who always seems to have a positive attitude and perseverance just radiating from them? Chances are, you are reading this book and identifying people who emulate these skills daily. Whoever that person is for you, spend as much time with them as you can. The positive you can gain from that time will have ripple effects for your school.

- **Invite others in.** If you have something great going on at lunch or after school, invite another person to join in. When you want to create a more positive workplace culture, take the time to invite others to the table. Building a positive culture can grow one invite at a time.

Say What You Mean in a Meaningful Way

When you lead authentically, it shows in your words. Every single one of them. Everything comes naturally, and you don't have to pretend or play the role you think others want you to play. Make sure your words, written and verbal, match the style of how you act. Remember the 73 percent principle? One week I messed up our weekly staff update. I had the wrong dates on upcoming events and wasn't transparent about sharing a task that had to be done by advisory teachers. Epic Fail. During a team meeting the next week, the final agenda item was, "What questions do you have for me?" Those errors came up, not as a gotcha but as a legitimate question about what I had meant.

Because I led as an authentic person willing to make mistakes, own them, learn from them, and lead better because of them, I didn't blame anyone else. Nor did I beat myself up for the error. I asked a clarifying question about how I could have been clearer, and thanked the team for helping me. Then I sent out a clarifying email and a brief apology.

Clarity in your communication grows over time. Seek support from others in improving and enhancing that soft skill. You'll also show others that you're working to grow and learn as a leader.

Had I not rolled out the carpet of transparency, authenticity, and servant leadership at the beginning of the year, and then sustained it throughout the year through my words and actions, I wouldn't have been able to laugh off that mistake—and the staff wouldn't have felt comfortable catching me in a mistake, and then correcting me.

Part of my leadership style is communicating in small groups instead of big meetings. I have always felt that large staff meetings lead to the sage-on-the-stage style of performance, and make it hard for me to read the staff and hard for them to share during deep conversations. My favorite place to connect and learn from teachers? PLC and team meetings. Every week, I rotated through PLC teams at the kindergarten center and grade-level teams at the middle school. The agenda was prepared ahead in our shared drive, and the template allowed for an open forum at the end. In this style, I have learned that the delivery changes with the team dynamic.

Recognizing the uniqueness of your audience allows you to change the delivery of your message as necessary, and allows time for them to share their ideas, concerns, and frustrations with you. I work to recap the meetings at the end of the week and decide which communication venue is essential for any follow-up tasks. Small group settings allow me to practice the message and tailor it to stakeholders to ensure that we are leading in the right way and in the right direction.

Just like in the game of *Frogger*, the path you take in leadership is not always a straight road. When you lead authentically, you become attuned to yourself and what your school needs. That might mean pausing on one initiative to push another one forward. You might have to redo a plan of implementation when it doesn't seem to be working. Leading in this way might also allow you to bring people from the outside in to support the work and help you with the focus and clarity in your communication. Having an additional adult with you during difficult conversations to give you feedback on your delivery and approach is also an opportunity to build skills such as listening and problem-solving.

Throughout all of this, however, the skill that matters most is honesty. Admit your mistakes, ask for forgiveness, and move forward. Wallowing in guilt and shame does no one any good, but leading and communicating with transparency, intentionality, and honesty? Well, that models a way to lead that everyone on the campus can identify with and demonstrate themselves.

LEADFORWARDSTRATEGY
Can You Hear Me Now? Build Your Communication Skills with Interaction and Action

- **Read, learn, and grow.** Just like our students, we will get better at leading and communicating when we learn about it. Grow your professional library with books and articles, and start following blogs and other leaders in and outside of education. Follow other leaders on social media channels to see their practice in daily action.

- **Seek feedback.** When you lead authentically, you ask for and receive feedback more readily. When you go into a situation, set your goals ahead of time for your communication and listening skills. Maybe you want to be a more active listener this time around, or be the last to sound off on a topic. Whatever your focus, ask someone in the meeting to give you feedback about how you implemented the skill, and then listen and use what they shared with you.

- **Reflect and renew.** Communicate with yourself as well. Reflect on your new learning. This work can take time and be a challenge. Start a journal. Pick an area of focus and list specific ways you want to build this muscle. Then down the road a month, a year, or longer, come back and look at where you started. You will find that you have grown, and you'll be able to see your biggest steps. What seemed hard is now seamless. And as always, document the work celebrations along the way. Find the space and time to reflect on your leadership style in theory and in action. Attend a conference or retreat, or create a weekend where you focus on and lean into your leadership style.

Stop Asking and Start Telling

So often our message can become lost in translation, and not just by the receiver, but by the sender. To create what you want, sometimes you have to state what you want in clear, non-negotiable terms. Here is an example: what if you have to create a new dismissal plan due to construction on the street that starts today? Asking twenty teachers what they think the path should be will mean thirty different ideas, and probably a few hurt feelings if you don't pick a specific one. Instead of asking for ideas, communicate a clear and focused message. In an email, memo, and probably announcement to ensure everyone hears it, state that due to construction outside of the school, you are changing your dismissal plan for the next few days. The new map is in everyone's mailbox and posted by the exit door. If there are questions you will be available after school. Make sure to thank everyone in advance for the flexibility in changing plans and recognize that in the big picture, this is a minor detail. But for one staff member, this could be a big deal.

I used to ask more than I told—until I realized how confusing that got for everyone. I wasted everyone's time asking for ideas on something I had already decided on. For example, let's say everyone needs to turn in peer observation documentation by a specific date. Which way of asking for this is the clearest:

- I know everyone is busy at this time of year. When you get a chance, could you please turn in your peer observations to me?

- Peer observations are due on Friday, April 23. Please turn them in electronically or put a paper copy in my office. Thank you.

Use caution when you use the word *please* with a directive. While it can be considered a polite way of asking for something, it can also be confused as a question instead of a request—an option rather than a requirement. It lacks a timeline or deadline. If you are asking a teacher to please get their grades in, do you know what they heard? Did you just tell them or infer to them that they can turn them in any time in the next year, when their peers are doing it by tomorrow? How confusing for them, and frustrating for you!

One word can make all the difference when talking with other people. Your words matter—how you say them, which ones you use, and the timing of when you use them.

During a meeting with community agencies, I remember asking another staff member if I could stay and attend the next part of the meeting. One of the community partners looked at me and asked, "Why are you asking to stay at a meeting in the building you lead?" Great question.

Many leaders started as teachers, and being assertive with adults is an ongoing struggle. We perceive being confident as being pushy and bossy, when being assertive is about leading the pack, advocating for others, and doing whatever it takes to meet the needs of your staff, school, and students. With that lens in mind, work toward being assertive without being a know-it-all.

Asking questions, being visible, and seeking input are three key ways to become assertive in your work, without pushing a perceived personal agenda. Connecting with your stakeholders with authenticity builds relationships and establishes your commitment to the goal. Again, communication graces take time, focus, and clarity. And when done well, they will move your school, committee, and team forward faster and in a more focused direction.

LEADFORWARDSTRATEGY
If the Message Is That Important, Work to Find a Way to Say It

- **Write it down.** It might be in your weekly newsletter, your staff memo, or in a letter to families. Before you send it, write it down and read and reread it. Clear communication requires time for rereading. Look to see if there are any unclear comments or directives in the notes. If it is important, *please* say it in more than one way (see earlier discussion about "please").

- **Ask for advice.** I have a go-to editor at our school. She has an incredible talent for just flipping a few words around to make a message 50 percent clearer than I had written it in the first place. Soft skill development doesn't have to occur in isolation. Look outside of yourself to find someone else to review what you wrote to ensure it is saying what you want to say.

- **Read the audience.** By getting to know your stakeholders, you get to know the best ways to send a message. For example, an announcement over the intercom directing staff to check email due to an unexpected early release will get more responses than just hitting send on the email and hoping people open it up in time. Survey your families; if the majority of them use Facebook to check on school updates, use it along with school-issued communication systems. It never hurts to send the same message via a few different communication channels. It increases the opportunity for everyone to hear it. Leading with the soft skill of focused and clear communication isn't a one-and-done situation, but an organic process of trying a few different platforms for the same message to find the right fit for the receivers.

- **Watch out for Minnesota Nice.** Don't say something beautiful on paper or in person, and then change your narrative behind the receiver's back. Be clear with your intentions and directions and watch the results match the message. No passive aggression needed.

Be Assertive, Not Aggressive:
The Art of Communication

When someone asks where you want to go to dinner, are you the type who answers, "Whatever you want is fine," when you actually have something specific in mind? Or worse yet, when you go to the restaurant you didn't want to go to, do you complain about everything from the service to the dessert? Communicating what you want can be done without forcing your agenda on someone else, or saying nothing and complaining about it along the way. Sometimes communication isn't about what you are trying to say, but what the other person hears. Utilize your skills of observation and reflection, and approach communication in a way that builds your ability to both speak and listen. Actively listening to another person requires you to be in the right space in your head and your heart.

Communicating well with others also means you must recognize when you are, and when you are not, in the right space to listen. One of my least favorite phrases in leadership is this: "Got a minute?" This usually comes while I am in the middle of an important email, picking up the phone to make an urgent call, or right after a stressful meeting while my heart is still racing. As a people pleaser, I almost always say yes to this request, and almost always immediately regret agreeing. My head is probably still in the last meeting, in the email, or in the introduction to the phone call I was about to make. Now that my internal agenda has been forcibly changed, my inner calm is disrupted. All of a sudden, I am wondering how this minute is going to affect the rest of my day and how many other things will be delayed, and because of it what is coming home with me on my overflowing plate.

It is better to say, "Could we talk about this later?" than it is to allow a conversation to continue when you are not in a space to listen and respond. When I am ready to listen, I can slide away from my desk, disengage from the computer screen, and put my phone at least arm's reach away. Turning away from technology and distraction signals to the other person that you are present and ready to hear what they have to say. Multitasking diminishes the other person's voice, as you are trying to prioritize what a person is saying over the multiple notifications coming through on your devices. Sometimes I even ask the other person to take a seat while I walk out of the office to refill my water bottle or get a little fresh air and reset my mind before our conversation.

Recalibrating my mind allows me to focus on what is in front of me rather than rehashing what just happened over and over in my mind. Taking intentional steps to clear your mind of clutter allows you to focus on what is ahead and what they are saying while they are sitting with you—which makes you a more worthwhile leader, and a better communicator.

LEAD**FORWARD**STRATEGY
How to Listen

Listening well means being in a space, place, and emotional state that allows you to be the sender or receiver of a message. People's time is valuable, yours included, so it is important to keep these ideas in mind.

- **Leaders, put your phones away.** Put it on silent, or better yet, give it to someone else outside of the room if it distracts you too much. Establishing a trusting relationship with the other person means that you are prioritizing their conversation over a possible telemarketing phone call.

- **Reset.** Sometimes when I walk down the hall, I take three deep breaths and move my hands and arms in an inhale/exhale motion. Visually and intentionally modeling mindfulness helps me redirect my thoughts toward the next task while releasing any energy from what might have just happened. Ensuring that I am ready to enter the next interaction is almost as crucial as listening to what the other person is saying.

- **Sometimes you don't have a minute.** I can tell you that I *have* sometimes found myself saying no, as in, "I don't have a minute right now." If I am racing between meetings and taking this call or conversation will make me late for something I have scheduled, it shows a lack of respect for my time and the person waiting for me. If it is that important, the person who wants to talk to me can make an appointment. That way they're guaranteed my full focus rather than a scattered version. If you don't have time, let the other person know that you do want to have the conversation, but because it is crucial, you want to make sure you have enough time to discuss and process.

It's Not About What They Say, But How You Respond

My inherent nature is to be a little dramatic. I can overanalyze anything and become overdramatic in a moment's notice. For the most part, this character flaw has worked in my favor; I can see how something small can seem impossible to a seventh-grader, and can use this skill to my advantage and walk them down off the cliff of awfulizing, worry, fret, and fear. However, this same overdramatic, unrealistic, and often irrational thinking and speaking can come at me from anyone: teachers, parents, students, and the central office. We all reach our breaking point; the one final thing tips us right over. Whatever the analogy, the experience is overwhelming, frustrating, and make us feel helpless. And most often, the person who pays is the one closest to us when we reach that breaking point.

As a leader who is considered honest, trustworthy, authentic, kind, dedicated, honorable, and any other characteristic that aligns with successful leadership, you most likely will end up on the receiving end of one of these rants. Sometimes it is on the phone, in the hallway, in a meeting, or in the community. Regardless of location, the outburst may include yelling, unrealistic statements, and heightened energy from the sender of the message. Communicating with someone in this state requires a heightened state of grace in the response. If you come back at them with the same energy, tone, and voice volume, chances are the conversation will head south quickly.

My first piece of advice is to do the opposite of your natural tendency. If your first instinct is to rebut or argue with the other person, try rephrasing what they are saying to you to offer clarity. If the tone of the message is loud, abrasive, and harsh, come back at them with a soft, slow tone of voice. When you walk into a situation and the other person is visibly escalated, pacing the room, and radiating an energy level that is through the roof, sit down and model calm energy to bring them down to your level. Before any genuine resolution to the conflict can happen, everyone needs to be in a state of peace. Otherwise, no one is going to be able to listen or discuss.

This outcome might not occur on the first try, but don't give up. Try a different mode of communication. If the initial interaction happened on the phone, invite them to follow up in person. If they stormed out of your classroom or office or left late for work, call them after their shift is done for the day and circle back to make sure they are okay. And always be ready with a sincere apology for any aspect of the interaction you can own. This will help diffuse a situation and get you both on a semi-equal playing field.

Assess the environment, read the room, and get ready to engage in conflict knowing that soft skills are sometimes those that can be seen and felt, not just heard out of the other person's mouth.

LEAD**FORWARD**STRATEGY
Read the Room and Prepare the Table

Setting up the space to have the conversation sends the message that this is important and safe, and assures the other party that you intend to build a trusting relationship. In times of high stress or conflict, offer the other person a safe space for communication, and you will get to the root of the problem.

- **Offer space**. Have the meeting in a calm, safe space. Windows and natural light can offer a quiet space. If the situation started in one area or hallway and is starting to escalate, ask for a break and have everyone walk to a new space. Fresh air and movement might help recalibrate the conversation.

- **Get them a glass of water**. I learned this one from my therapist. When I come upon a physical interaction or fight between students, once I have everyone in a safe, separate space, if one of the parties is still aggravated, I will give them a glass of water. This strategy starts to slow their breathing and brings their heart rate down. After a while, I will notice their energy level coming down, and then the conversation about what happened can begin.

- **Apologize**. It never hurts to be a human in these inter-actions. Saying you're sorry sincerely diffuses the con-flict quickly.

MOVING**FORWARD**

Communicating is essential in our life and work, and understanding yourself at every moment will help you ensure that your communication is clear and compelling. Too often, our best intentions are met with questions and frustration, not because of what we said, but because of how or when we said it. Communication and grace are simple; they are both about you, and not about you. A key to ensuring the conversation goes well is to make sure you are in the right physical and emotional space. When you are stressed, frustrated, or overwhelmed, chances are you might unload on the other person instead of gently easing into the conversation.

> *Your state of mind matters as much as the words you speak.*

Just as important is ensuring that your partner in the conversation is ready to hear. Asking if this is a good time, and listening to their response, shows that you care about their state and want them to be ready to receive the communication. Being transparent, upfront, honest, and genuine shows the other person that while they might not agree with what you say, it's coming from a place of honesty and integrity.

Listening well means reducing the static in your mind in terms of assumptions. Don't assume the worst, but expect the best of others and what they are thinking and saying. Too often, our heads get us into more drama than necessary and it distracts us from the real work of relationships.

Communicating well is not easy; it takes practice and a lot of humility. Reflecting on what was said, how it was said, and whether your state of mind or the timing of the conversation influenced it, are all important in your learning and leading journey. As you move forward in this work, create a journal of communication reflections so you can go back and learn from past conversations. And remember that your state of mind matters as much as the words you speak.

CHAPTER 5
LEAD**FORWARD**JOURNAL

Growing the good

List the names of staff, students, and/or families who I can write a note of gratitude to this week.

_____

_____

_____

Before I address a situation or circumstance in which I am frustrated, I need to find the common ground or a compliment to share to start the conversation on a positive point. Write down what I could say.

_____

_____

_____

Just walk away

What space in my school or in my personal life is causing me stress and becoming too toxic to handle?

_____

_____

_____

How could I lead with grace and move away from that space?

_____

_____

_____

Sharing what you know

Who and what am I reading to grow in gratitude and to grow in my authentic leadership style?

_____

_____

_____

_____

_____

How am I sharing that knowledge with others?

_____

_____

_____

Which of these ideas do I like best: book quotes on social media, book clubs, intentional conversations around the book, blog, vlog, or a different idea?

_____

_____

_____

_____

_____

_____

Share your journal entries and ideas at #LeadForward on Twitter.

CHAPTER 6

Grace in Relationships

Interact with Manners, Mindfulness, and Meaning

You can disagree without being disagreeable.
— RUTH BADER GINSBURG, SUPREME COURT JUSTICE

RACE IN RELATIONSHIPS is best defined as rolling up your sleeves and getting into the dirt of the work. People are complicated. We are not an algorithm you can run through a supercomputer that turns over the perfect way to respond. Timing, tone, and relationships have more to do with how the message is received than what you say. One of the toughest lessons to learn in this work is to determine what you want out of a relationship and to maintain that focus. Too often we get caught up in being friends, being liked, or other external influences, and forget that caring about others sometimes means we have to address things that won't be liked—but these things are needed.

Everything you do is your responsibility: yes.
Everything you do is always your fault: no.

You make difficult decisions that leave an impact every day. Some days that impact is positive, other days it is not, and at times it is just neutral. Grace in relationships requires you to own your actions while letting go of what you can't control. In this work, accessing your ability to build healthy interpersonal skills while setting boundaries is the grace that elevates the school culture to the next level. Modeling how to be a team player is not the same as being the team's punching bag. Leaving gossip behind and letting go of the need to win the popular vote will allow you to lead with your authentic self. And honestly, when you walk away and let go of what others "might" be saying, it shows them that you will respond the same way regardless of whether it's a light day or a dark one.

Likes or Leadership?

Taking a new path or position can be an exciting time in your career. Moving schools, switching grade levels, or transitioning from the classroom into a different role can be a fresh start, a reboot, or a reminder of why you were called into this service.

And while there are many positives to making these changes, one transition became the highest and lowest place in my career. I entered a setting ready to face new challenges and armed with years of experience. While I didn't know the players, I understood the positions they were in and the skills necessary to be successful. I walked in with my historically optimistic attitude and high expectations and worked with a team to change the course of an organization. I walked beside staff who elevated their performance almost immediately with little to no coaching. Just explicit permission to do what they knew was right for those they served. Students who, in previous years, felt isolated and undervalued, stepped up to take leadership positions, and we saw increased classroom participation and performance alongside decreased office behavioral referrals. Community opinion was high, and parent concerns were down. This year was turning into the best year of my career ... until it wasn't anymore.

For the 99 percent of stakeholders that were on board, supportive, and thriving in this new leadership era, there was a 1 percent that set forth to consume 90 percent of my time and thoughts. At first, there were minor hiccups: deadlines missed, concerns not addressed. A few staff started to intentionally and unintentionally undermine the vision. It's possible they had insecurities about how to transition to fit the needs of our stakeholders. Staff from other buildings started to verbally attack teachers in the school because of their change in attitude and new teaching perspective. Hurtful comments came out, such as, "Why are you trying so hard with those kids" or "They are going to wreck the rest of your class, you should just kick them out." Teachers felt under fire and looked to the leader for help.

At the same time, an epically fictional narrative was being written as truth. A shift was happening, and the bubble wrap I had delicately placed around the staff, families, and students was in danger of ripping and tearing, leading to damage for those I cared most deeply about.

At this point in the story, I was pushed into the deep, dark valley from the view high atop the mountain. Emails, accusations, comments, and phone calls overwhelmed my day. Investigations, reports, and accounts now had to be documented and filed, and consumed time that would have been better spent in the classrooms and halls of the school. I noticed the impact on my health. I had a harder time sleeping, less motivation to engage with friends, and an appetite that was up and down. I lost my running shoes for four months. Doors were locked, literally and figuratively, and I retreated into my negative thoughts and awfulized other aspects of my life and leadership instead of limiting that negativity to the one area under fire.

The pit turned into a den that had no light at the end.

At this time, I made my biggest mistake. I went from professional to personal. I took every comment, every email, every meeting, as an attack on who I was rather than what I was doing. I panicked every time specific staff sent emails. I isolated myself from those I usually confided in, feeling shame and guilt over this situation. I struggled to sleep, eat, and focus on things outside of this stressor, and became a shell of the self I had tried so hard to build.

At a pivotal point in the year, I had signed up to attend a conference with other educators from across the state. As the weekend came up, I started to devise excuses as to why I didn't need to attend. An awkward conversation with a staff member occurred right before I was supposed to leave, a snowstorm hit, and traffic was bad enough that it would have been easier to go home and go to bed until Monday. Thanks to an incredible support team at home, who pushed me out the door, I showed up, bruised and cautious about sharing any part of my story with a room full of strangers. It didn't take long to realize I wasn't alone. In small and big ways, the other educators shared their own stories of being in the pit and the den—some significantly worse than my own. I asked for help. I received support from others and made connections that I carry forward.

I went back into the den on Monday, equipped with a new narrative. This season would not define me. Why I got into the work at the beginning was tarnished, but still present. And I started to reach out and ask others for help, support, and guidance. Slowly, the light began to shine through, and our persistence paid off. What I learned from that time of life was how to set boundaries with others' opinions and behaviors, and how to let their baggage go so I could focus on what needed to grow.

Be careful not to awfulize everything based upon one interaction, a few emails, or a decision that went sideways. Look at the big picture and seek perspective—as well as advice from your team.

Relationships and communication work together, and when communication works, relationships get stronger. When communication fails, relationships falter. That doesn't mean all conversations are sunshine and bubbles. The tough conversations were not easy, but they were necessary to keep my vision in sight and to frame the perspective that I didn't need to own the responses of others or fear listening to their feedback. Those relationships allowed all of us to hold each other accountable and build soft skills such as being team players. Through this season, some relationships became stronger while some dissolved. I came out of it with a few additional scars, and more wisdom to share with others about how they don't need to walk into the pit alone.

LEAD**FORWARD**STRATEGY
Keep It Professional

You may work in a middle school, but that doesn't give you permission to act like a teenager. Sidebar comments and sabotaging might lead you to change your decisions based upon what you think others think of you. That challenges your integrity and diminishes your ability to lead authentically. Fight back by building relationships and making yourself vulnerable. Utilize honesty, kindness, and care, and you will find that you never have to walk into that pit of doubt alone again.

- **It is not always about you.** Although you may feel personally attacked, don't personalize other people's comments about how you lead and teach. Maybe you saw someone's eye roll. Or perhaps someone came to you and said someone else was talking about you. When you are transitioning to a new position or trying a new idea, you might lose confidence and fall back into old habits that do not help build up new relationships. If you keep it professional, chances are the other person will too.

- **Don't go dark.** It is hard not to retreat when you feel like everything around you is caving in. Be careful not to awfulize everything based upon one interaction, a few emails, or a decision that went sideways. Look at the big picture and seek perspective—as well as advice from your team—instead of assuming everyone is out to get you. You might not see the whole picture, and going dark will keep you from asking for advice from those who can see more clearly than you.

- **Find a friend.** The worst thing you can do when things go wrong is to refuse to ask for help. Find a friend and talk with them about what happened. Chances are, they can offer perspective and give you the flashlight you need to see through the dark.

Deflective Versus Reflective Leadership

Working through the dirt and mud requires strength and courage. What you must decide in every relationship and hard conversation is whether you will deflect or reflect what you need to say. When frustrated with someone else, do you immediately look to that person's flaws without considering any faults you could have brought into the mix? Are you more apt to drag out the conversation, waiting for it to dissolve before you have to say anything, and hoping it doesn't get worse or get someone hurt in the meantime?

Relationships require effort and a willingness to meet in the middle. That could mean stepping back and letting the other person share their hurt or frustration about the interaction. It could mean stepping up and recognizing that your tone or the words you used caused pain or frustration that fractured the relationship, and you have a responsibility to fix it. I am not a fan of conflict, seriously not a fan. I can tell when an awkward conversation is coming up; my nerves get the better of my right hand and me. When in that situation, or leading up to it, my right hand shakes terribly. I tend to lose focus on other tasks right before these situations, and can be short with others because my head is full of the scenarios that could play out. And speaking of speaking, I struggle to speak without my voice shaking, and my verbal vomit comes out in full effect. So no, I don't like to have these conversations. But I know I can't delegate them to others, either. Leading with grace and building deep relationships means moving past the nice conversations or fear of having the tough talks. While it is hard at the moment, it is necessary for the long term.

I have learned over and over again that the spray-and-pray approach to difficult conversations is never successful. Going into a staff room and telling everyone to get to work on time will only cause stress for the staff who might be late one time in five years due to a significant circumstance. The ones who are chronically late will continue to roll in that way. Building strong relationships with others means you might have to say something that others have been afraid to say—and you might have to say it in an awkward conversation with one person.

Deflecting and reflecting doesn't just apply when you are the sender of the message, but also when you are the receiver. When people approach you with a concern or error, do you deflect blame to others, or do you recognize your role and thank the person for bringing it to your attention? As I mentioned in Chapter 3, in my years as an autism teacher, we created social stories and cartoons all the time. I became a pro at drawing stick figures on whiteboards to represent two parties in a conversation or conflict. In social cartoons, there were two types of communication: thought bubbles and talk bubbles. Now I use this analogy when it comes to receiving information. When someone brings up an idea, compliment, concern, or conversation topic that requires a response, you have a filter: your thought bubble. Use that area for your initial thoughts, sarcastic comments, or unproductive statements that would have zero impact on the conversation. As long as you don't pop the thought bubble, you keep those thoughts in your head and prevent them from coming out as hurtful or harsh words.

It's a saving grace to recognize that you don't have to say everything you believe, and I use it all the time. You can share your thought bubble with a safe person or, like Abraham Lincoln did, write those thoughts down and never send them. No matter how much we want to say something, the truth is that it might not change the situation. Often, those thoughts have to do with wanting to be right, rather than wanting to resolve an issue. The idea of a thought bubble is to protect both you and the other person in the conversation and to continue to build a healthy and trusting relationship without side comments and unproductive responses.

Having an open door practice toward others also includes having an open mind and grace when it comes to your response. Others will stop coming to you with ways to improve the school if you continuously complain or blame others for the ideas not being implemented already. And be careful to shut the door immediately after someone opens it. While the initial idea they share might be a little far-fetched or outrageous, the person took the time to share it. Be sincere and gracious about recognizing this. Wait until they're finished sharing before you start responding with your (appropriate) thoughts.

LEADFORWARDSTRATEGY
Push the Pause Button

Grace in relationships requires a check of your self-regulation. Are you in the right place and space to have the conversation? While you can't control the reactions of people, you can control your response and preparedness.

- **Are you ready to engage and respond?** Check your emotional state before you attempt to engage in a conversation. And if you must have the conversation right at that moment, let the other person know why you might be a little off or upset at the start.

  For example, if you had a time scheduled to meet and discuss a difficult situation, and right before that meeting you had a difficult interaction with a student, you might start the meeting by pointing out the elephant in the room. I have made statements such as, "I am sorry if I am off. The interaction I had right before our meeting has me a little out of balance." Another good one is, "What we are about to discuss is difficult and I will do my best to be clear and concise, but if I am not, please let me know. I can repeat any part." Leading with vulnerability in your relationships allows you to be real and honest upfront and build better relationships with those you're leading.

- **Write it down.** Take time to write down what you want to say, then review it and even read it aloud. Reflect on the situation to make sure you're ready to engage in productive discourse, not harmful assaults. Taking the time to prepare yourself will help you maintain the relationship rather than harming it with hastily spoken, unrehearsed words.

- **Be on, not ornery.** If you are agitated or frustrated, pause and reschedule the meeting. If your energy doesn't support the conversation you are going to have, it will be hard to be successful.

- **Watch out for the spray and pray.** Successful conversations create change when they are directed at the right source. Saying something to everyone and hoping "the one" hears it is an ineffective strategy. Take the time to connect with the specific people who are causing the concern, and you will be more productive and build trust across all stakeholders.

No matter how well you prepare, how much time you give, or how hard you try, you cannot manipulate, control, or direct the responses of others. What you can do is model what you want to see from others.

Focus on What You Can Control

I used to take weeks before I initiated a difficult conversation because I was afraid of what others would say. In my error, I forgot the most important point: it wasn't how I said it, but the fact that it needed to be said, and as a leader, it was my job to get it done.

Leading with grace doesn't mean you will be liked. Leading with grace in relationships *does* mean you will build a sense of trust with stakeholders—as long as you act authentically and keep your word. You can never control the reactions of others. No matter how well you prepare, how much time you give, or how hard you try, you cannot manipulate, control, or direct the responses of others. What you *can* do is model what you want to see from others. When you are leading with grace, you can and must care about people. That doesn't mean you can control the narrative they spin when they're talking to others. It's important to realize that, and to let go of what you can't control and focus on the things you can.

To lead with grace in this way, you must be good in your own mental space. When responding to attacks or looking into a week of tough conversations, make sure you have taken the extra effort for self-care. What can you control? Are you focused on that? Have you left work at reasonable hours? And once you pulled away, did you turn email off for the rest of the day? Are you eating, sleeping, and exercising the stress away via healthy outlets? When the stress and challenges become too much, have you sought professional help to navigate the rough seas? Ensuring that you are well allows you to engage in the tough work in safe ways—and leads to better success for you and your relationships with others.

When I taught a coding class with kindergartners, we talked about the two roles of pair programmers: driver and navigator. The driver was the one actually at the controls, while the navigator was giving advice and looking at the bigger picture without actually touching the keyboard. When we are working on building skills in developing relationships, how often do we blur those roles? We set out to be the navigator, and then when the other person isn't doing it as accurately as we wish, we jump in (or over them) and take the controls. When delegating tasks and responsibilities, do you give it over entirely ... or go back and look over another's shoulder, picking at how they are doing it? Setting boundaries with grace means we know how and when to let go and how to adjust our responses.

LEAD**FORWARD**STRATEGY
Know Your Role

- **Move forward.** Not everyone is going to like you, particularly when you conduct tough conversations. Yes, at times, you will lose a friend or get into a war of words with someone close. When that happens, give it time and reevaluate the relationship. How did they react to the need for that conversation? Was the conversation necessary? Did it move the school forward? If it was, and if it did, then you did the right thing and need to move forward from the fight or lost relationship.

- **Whose job is it anyway?** Just because someone else blows up or messes up doesn't mean you have to get involved or try to solve the problem or situation. Try hard not to insert yourself into problems that are not yours to solve. The more you blur lines, micromanage, or attempt to swoop in and solve problems, the more complicated the conversations and decisions can get, and the more work for everyone. You cannot lead successfully if you overextend yourself and try to take everyone's problems onto your shoulders. Fill your role and allow others to fill theirs so everyone stays in their lane.

Doors and Doormats

The summer before my senior year of high school, I was crowned Miss Congeniality for the Northland Mardi Gras festival in Ladysmith, Wisconsin. I still have the sash, buttons, and many memories from that experience. For me, the recognition was an honor higher than winning the title of Queen or first runner-up, as Miss Congeniality was voted on by all the other contestants and given to the one who was the most friendly during the week. I always prided myself on being the person who didn't want anyone to sit alone at the lunch table. The person who was friends with everyone and opened the door to anyone who needed it.

After college, I realized that opening the door for others can also mean opening myself up to being someone's doormat. The person who always says "Yes, of course," or "How can I help?" can also be taken advantage of more quickly than others. A few people started to figure out that I would do their work for them, stay late, come early, or listen for hours as they shared things that had happened to them. In these interactions, I left defeated and drained, no longer feeling welcomed, but used.

I struggle with being an open door for others without being a doormat. I want to be welcoming, helpful, encouraging, and supportive. I don't want to be taken advantage of in my efforts. Establishing clear boundaries with others is essential to maintaining sanity and respectfully building safe, trusting relationships. This is just as important as nurturing relationships, because it keeps everyone in their lane, and helps you maintain your mental and emotional well-being.

One way to establish boundaries is to define your role in the relationship. Are you trying to be a coach or a controller? Another way you can move from being the doormat to the open door is through honesty. Too often, we wait, withhold, or only partially inform others of what is bothering us, as we don't want to hurt their feelings. We don't tell them when we're feeling used. This causes tension and sometimes distance in relationships, because we start to pull away—without telling them why we're doing it.

To build strength in the area of honesty and timeliness, employ a no-excuses execution. Write down what you need to say, and then around it, write all the reasons you haven't said it yet. Look at the excuses and start to cross them off if they aren't grounded in anything tangible. Suddenly, you will see the actual barriers to confrontation. Now you can deal with them swiftly and recalibrate the relationship to one of honesty and timeliness. Stop holding a grudge for past behaviors; if you didn't address them, you can't hold the other person responsible. Chances are good that they didn't even know what they were doing to upset you.

A fine line exists between being an open door and being someone's doormat. When you lead with grace in relationships, you realize that you not only have to recognize boundaries but also use them.

LEADFORWARDSTRATEGY
Set Personal and Professional Boundaries

- **Set a boundary.** It is great to be a friend, but you don't have to be anyone's everything. You certainly don't have to solve all their problems or take on all their responsibilities, especially if it ends up hurting your ability to do your job of leading. Say no to requests that will take time and space away from your own needs, and set boundaries about how often you can and will help other people.

- **Check the lock.** Once you've set a specific boundary, make sure you are consistent with your response. Saying yes "this one time" gives the other person a mixed message. Instead, stay true to the boundaries you set early on.

- **Shake it out**. If a person is asking something of you too often or pushing your boundaries regularly, it might be time to set stronger boundaries, or even eliminate the relationship. Evaluate this relationship. What are you getting from it? If you struggle to find anything, and the person is taking more from you than they're giving in return, it might be time to gently end it.

- **Don't be a stranger**. Just because a boundary has been set doesn't mean you must avoid interactions or feel awkward in your communications with that person. If you avoid them, they might start to think that you're angry with them, when you're just maintaining a

healthy relationship. Circle back to that person intentionally and interact normally with them—within your
boundaries. Don't sacrifice the relationship just because
you've had to build boundaries.

Poke Holes in It

Too often when leading, we think that others expect us to produce
our best ideas and perfect products on the first attempt. Even worse
is the fact that we come to expect that perfection of *ourselves*.

To combat the perfection syndrome, we must lead with the soft
skills of transparency and collaboration. We must allow our vulnerability to shine through and ask others for their insight, ideas, and
help. In short, we must prove that we are not perfect and that we
need our team to support us if we're going to succeed. One strategy
I learned was to ask others to poke holes in my ideas. I learned
that if I came with a plan and asked others to see themselves in
it and tell me what was missing, I ended up with a much better
result. We also had stronger buy-in from the team because they
had helped to come up with the ultimate plan.

At one school, we had these great end-of-quarter celebrations.
When they first started, I tried to plan them myself—the activities,
the schedule, the rotations, the criteria, and the communication. It
was like I was planning every detail of my wedding while trying
to walk down the aisle. It was exhausting and I became more frustrated when people gave me feedback than if I had been in a better
state. This was the opposite of productive.

After two rounds of planning in isolation, I decided to try the
poke-holes-in-it strategy. I came up with a skeleton of a plan where
we were going to go off-site for a game day at our local sports
dome. I had the time frame for the bus, I knew which staff members were going to be able to supervise, and I knew the criteria for

qualifying. One month before the event, I started to meet with the teachers every week to map out the plan. What activities, materials, and other details did we need to make this successful? Each week, I came back to an energetic group of teachers who had come up with activities and station rotations. They even added in music and a board game section for students who wanted to sit and watch, and not play in one of the competitive games. That day ended up being better than it would have been if I'd insisted on planning it by myself. Students had a great time, staff enjoyed it, and I had an opportunity to walk around and ask questions to garner ideas for minor improvements the next year. I was no longer frustrated at the feedback but instead was honored that the stakeholders took the time to think more deeply about what we were offering.

Leading with grace in these circumstances requires a deep level of vulnerability. Being open to feedback tells your team that you need their help, and will listen and use it. Strong leaders are not built in isolation but in moments of problem-solving and trust. Whether the project involves the school handbook, back-to-school conferences, or future professional development, ask early on what you are missing and seek help in making sure it is the best for all involved.

LEAD**FORWARD**STRATEGY
Bring People Along to Create the Best Plan

Building a team requires energy, effort, and a willingness to involve others so you can make the best decisions with the most information. Use your soft skills of communicating, asking questions, and getting clarification to make sure you build the best and most team-oriented plan possible.

- **Ask early and often**. Present the idea early and with as much background information as you can, then ask for help and advice. Ask team members what they would change and how they can help. Bringing them in early ensures that they get to help you build the plan, and this increases buy-in.

- **Don't ask questions if you already know the answer.** If there are non-negotiables (budget, bussing, parental permissions), make sure the team has the information. Be transparent with the items you already have answers to, and keep the team focused on the items that need their help and advice.

- **Circle back with the feedback.** After the event, bring the team back together to reflect and make notes for future ideas. What went well during the event? What could have used more work? Was the timeline right? Could you have involved more people for a better result? Discussing this right after the event will help you build a plan for the next event while the previous one is still fresh in the team's mind.

MOVING**FORWARD**

I used to be afraid of lunch supervision. Let's do the math: 250 sixth- through eighth-graders plus one of me equals thirty minutes of pure anxiety. As an assistant principal of a middle school, lunchroom supervision was my responsibility. It wasn't a joyful one. I would look forward to shorter school days because they meant less lunch duty. Every two weeks, I had an off-site meeting that meant I missed lunch duty on those days as well. In short, lunch was the least favorite part of my day.

Then a strange thing happened when I went to lead at an elementary school; I learned to love lunch duty. Watching parents come in, and the excitement on everyone's face when they sat down with the class to eat, was priceless. The energy of the cafeteria also went up when I went into the room, unlike my middle school experience where students would ignore my presence. These kindergarten students missed me when I was absent! I was spoiled with so many hugs, smiles, and waves when I came in that it was hard *not* to spend time in the lunchroom. I loved the interactions with students and families. Many days, I walked out of the cafeteria smiling, with maple syrup stuck to my sweater and ketchup on my pants from eager students wanting to hug me.

Fast forward to coming back to that middle school. Even though as the principal I was no longer responsible for lunch duty, you would still find me in the lunchroom at least two to three times a week. I replaced my previous anxiety with optimism. Each day, I was surprised at what student waved me over to sit down and start up a conversation. I learned a lot about fantasy football picks, the right hair extensions, and everything in between. I began to serve, supervise, and clean up that cafeteria regularly, with a smile.

So what changed? Not the kids, not the room. Just my attitude. When you approach each challenge as an opportunity to learn and grow while leading in your authentic way, things change. I learned to look at all of those potential relationships, and let them come to me. Are there still kids who ignore me when I walk into the room? Yes, but now all I see are the ones who are smiling and waving, which outnumber the other few. Loving what you do and doing what you love means you find joy and relationships in the smallest tasks. Serving others and stepping outside of your office and role expands others' perception of you. Leading as a learner and servant shows that you are fulfilling a mission, building a positive school culture, and creating strong relationships with others—one lunch duty at a time.

I learned that finding grace in relationships is about finding joy in the mundane tasks. By cultivating significance in the day-to-day operations, I learned to love them—even lunch duty. Step outside of your comfort zone, kick the box out of the way that you have been standing on for years, and elevate your interactions with others one opportunity at a time. Lead forward in your way, and love every situation that presents itself, even the unexpected ones.

CHAPTER 6
LEADFORWARDJOURNAL

Likes or leadership

In what circumstance or situation am I dragging my feet on making a decision because of hurt feelings?

_____

_____

_____

_____

_____

Why is it important to push through the discomfort and lean into making the right call or having the hard conversation?

_____

_____

_____

_____

Ready, set, write

Think of an upcoming difficult conversation. Before engaging in it, write down what I want to say, and if possible, practice with a mentor.

_____

_____

_____

_____

Share your journal entries and ideas at #LeadForward on Twitter.

CHAPTER 7

Social Graces
Interact and Act Online

*We don't have a choice on whether we do social
media, the question is how well we do it.*
— Erik Qualman, Speaker and Author of
*Socialnomics: How Social Media Transforms
the Way We Live and Do Business*

In today's world, we should give badges to those who successfully navigate social media and technology. The days are gone when someone could be mad at you without you knowing about it, because they only tell a friend or spouse. Now, with smartphones and 24/7 access to communication channels, problematic conversations have much bigger audiences. How can you have a vulnerable conversation with another person when you are not in the same physical space? How do you lead authentically when people can only see 280 characters of your point? Leading with grace means you must navigate the digital world as well. Increasingly, our relationships are developing and growing in the online space.

Leading, Not Losing, with Technology

I still remember it clearly. I was so angry, frustrated, and bothered by someone else's actions that I tried to vent to another teacher via my flip phone. I crafted a note like, "Seriously, are we going to have to do her work all year?" Not even a millisecond after I hit send, I realized I'd sent it to the person I was complaining about. Epic, epic fail.

Almost immediately, that person tried to call me, and I ignored the call. I was utterly embarrassed. Not only had I been caught, but I had turned into the person who did such a thing. Technology has completely changed how we speak to each other, and it doesn't seem to be getting any easier to navigate. I violated the first rule I shared with middle schoolers when they were exploring their voice on social media: "If you wouldn't say it to the other person's face, don't text or type it."

A post on your private Facebook page can ensure negative comments from friends and family, be it politics to what you are eating for dinner. It's all up for debate and discussion. I will be honest; I over-analyze everything I put on a social media platform. I am in the habit of asking my teenage boys before posting things so Grandma and Great-Grandma can see them, and wait for their "yes" before I post.

Authenticity in what you say, post, and retweet is a work in progress, and when you are online, you are always "on." Sharing your stories and using your voice is a tricky teeter-totter. Share too much? Not sharing enough? Posting every classroom activity or highlighting one? Posting a blog to your Facebook page or hiding in the cloud somewhere? Navigating the world from our fingertips instead of face to face has its challenges. However, this World Wide Web has exposed us to more ideas, more energy, and more collaboration than ever before. You can connect with other educators and leaders with similar interests and passions without waiting for a phone call, letter in the mail, or even an emailed response.

Almost ten years later, I remember that situation like it was yesterday. I still beat myself up for it—not just about what I said, but that I let another person's actions affect who I was as a person. Had I just taken thirty minutes (or even thirty seconds!) before I hit send, had I taken a walk, or waited to say something face to face ... the situation would have been so much better. Being on one side of the negative consequences of typing something that should have been a conversation instead has taught me that even though a quick tweet or comment is easier, it doesn't make it right. Leading with grace in an online world means taking the work you've been doing on authenticity, vulnerability, empathy, and integrity and using it to practice your self-restraint and self-regulation. Use those soft skills as filters for your words before you post them online. Keep that thought bubble in place, and protect yourself from the repercussions of speaking too plainly on social media.

LEADFORWARDSTRATEGY
Recovering from a Bad Tweet, Text, or Post

It happened. You commented on someone else's post about you or your school. That family relative who always has an inciting comment had one, and it hit you the wrong way. Maybe you had a difficult day at work and the first thing you saw on Facebook was a perfect picture of your high school friend hanging out with her friends, and having more fun than you *again*. In the spur of the moment, you posted a comment full of attitude, and later you wished no one had seen it. But they did. While the best option is to keep from doing it, our soft skills of integrity and vulnerability mean that when we mess up, we own it—and learn from it.

- **What did you do wrong, and how can you do better next time?** Navigating tools like texts and tweets is an entirely new arena. When you "reply all," send something to the wrong friend, or let your frustrations get the better of you, take the time to reflect and learn from what you did so you don't do it again. If you're about to do something, but have a gut feeling that it's not the right action, stop yourself. Call or ask someone in real time for their opinion before you post your comment for the whole world to see. Or take the advice I give seventh-graders: if you wouldn't say it to your grandma on Sunday, don't type and send it to someone else today.

- **Be careful of competition.** Just because someone else posted their dinner doesn't mean you have to as well. Think about why you want to share each picture. You do not need to compare your newsfeed to anyone else's, and if you start to, then take a break from social media until you can find your vision. Then start again.

- **Say you are sorry in real life, in real time.** Okay, so you made the mistake. Make sure to apologize, and if possible, do it face to face. Just two weeks ago, I accidentally sent a message to the entire school instead of one teacher. While it was nothing unprofessional or unkind, I still rushed to apologize. Owning your mistakes and being upfront with your apologies show the other person (or people) the possibility of grace in forgiveness.

Filter or Funnel: When to Speak, When to Stop

While observing in a science class the other week, I watched students use a funnel to pour liquid into a container with a small opening. When I asked the students why they were using the funnel, they replied, "So nothing spills over." That comment had me reflecting on the importance of using a funnel when responding to others through electronic communication. Our words are powerful; they can build bridges between people or build walls and cause frustration and hurt feelings. A filter on how you communicate a message can help you keep your own bias, frustration, or emotions to yourself. You can then ensure that the receiver hears what you have to say with neutrality.

But how do you apply that funnel?

Have you tried the "sleep on it" method? You take twelve hours, get rest, and then look once again at what someone else sent (or said). Too often, we want to get it done or get it off our plate, and we look back and realize a day later that the response could have been better, or even that the situation wasn't as terrible as it seemed. One way to support this approach is taking email off your devices and committing to not looking at it after a certain point in the evening. Our brains need rest and checking email late at night causes us to pick up our second shift of work at home and then struggle to shut it off. Responding and working late at night also affects the time we could have with our spouse, friends, family, and even ourselves. Instead, we are preoccupied with what we just read on our computer or phone. Trust me, no one says, "Wow, I wish I would have read that email late last night."

Take a walk. Seriously. There is such a thing as email apnea. It occurs when you hold your breath unconsciously while reading emails. In my study of this topic, I have also heard of people clenching their jaw, grinding their teeth, and increasing their unproductive and negative thoughts around the subject or sender of the email. You, like me, might have a short list of "trigger" senders and people who post to social media. It might be because of previous experience or your current stress level. When those senders come up, we know ahead of time that it's going to be a problem. Leading with grace means recognizing those triggers and creating strategies to support you through amicable interactions. Leading with grace also means knowing when to back off, and how to apply a filter when you do reply.

One of the best interventions is to immediately step away from the computer or put your email out of sight. Taking a tech timeout refocuses your attention on other things and helps you recalibrate and reassess the situation. I try to find something that brings me joy and to engage in that activity for a short period. Walking the halls and greeting students, sitting in a class and engaging with educators, or even just going outside and getting some fresh air helps me regain perspective on the circumstances. It allows me to return and craft a response that has a little less exaggeration and a little more professionalism.

Did you know that even Abraham Lincoln struggled with responding to others? In Doris Kearns Goodwin's book *Leadership in Turbulent Times*, she shares a story about Abraham Lincoln and his "hot letters." President Lincoln would write his frustration down and then never sign or send the letter! The art of getting it off your chest doesn't have to include sending it to someone else; it just needs to get out of your head.

If that approach was good enough for President Lincoln, why wouldn't it work for you? When you are preparing to respond to an accusation, a post, or a note from someone, try pen and paper first. Write your response down. Your first draft could be what I commonly refer to as my "middle school girl" draft. The one that is high on emotion and data, and possibly a tad unprofessional. Get it all out, seriously. Then let it go.

Review the letter you will never, ever send and assess how serious it is. See whether any parts are informative, factual, or worth addressing, and throw away the rest. Once you have reflected on your letter, shred it. Rip it up into a million pieces or run it through a shredder. This exercise was for you and you alone, and no one needs to see your deep, dark frustrations. Leading with grace in communications means sometimes filtering out your high-emotion responses before you can get to work. That grace shows others that you are leading with integrity and being the authentic you—without the drama.

LEAD**FORWARD**STRATEGY
Find Your Voice with Your Pen

Once you know what is bothering you, it is easier to find a graceful way to address others. Using the journal prompts in this chapter and applying the questions through the lens of an online world are ways for you to enhance your graceful responses to comments and questions.

- **What is the issue?** So what is truly bothering you about a person's post? Taking the time to reflect intentionally will allow you to work through whatever you think and feel in a private space.

- **Write a letter to shred.** It is too easy to reply, fire back, and watch the situation escalate if you respond immediately. Instead, use President Lincoln's approach, but don't send it, post it, or hit reply. Start writing a draft with pen and paper. Write down what you want to say, then seal it, lock it up, and come back to it later. Chances are, you'll realize that the process of writing was useful, even though you will shred the first version before deciding how to respond appropriately, or whether to respond at all.

- **Step away.** Okay, that person just sent you an email. Before you open it or start to awfulize what it says, go for a walk or do something else to reframe your mind. How you respond is based on your frame of mind at the moment. You can't control what they say, but you can control how you respond. Give yourself space.

159

Follow or Friend?

When you have unlimited options of who you can follow or friend, applying a filter becomes critically important. You need to make sure you're filling your social media feed with high-value characters. What about that person who posts just about everything? The one who has more selfies than posts about the work their students are doing? Presenting a perfectly painted picture is not the same as leading with vulnerability, and following such people won't necessarily add to your growth as a leader.

Find friends, mentors, and a team of leaders who have a connection to your work, and you will build your leadership skills and maintain your sanity at the same time. Jim Rohn said, "You are the average of the five people you spend the most time with." Use the following questions to start figuring out who you've already collected as your network—and what they might be teaching you when it comes to grace and authentic leadership.

- Who are the five people in the building I connect with?

- Who are the five people I text the most on my phone?

- Who are the five people I follow most closely on social media?

- What five podcasts do I listen to the most?

- What five books do I reference the most in my work?

- When I have a problem, who are the five people I am most likely to call first?

This is your professional (and sometimes personal) learning network, or PLN. Establishing and cultivating a PLN is essential to leading from a learner approach.

How do you build up that network on social media? Stop and think about that for a moment. Who in this work leads with the grace you want to exhibit? How can you find them, and how can you start learning from them? When I first started using Twitter and Voxer as professional development tools, I watched and listened, but didn't respond or reply right away. Just like in my daily interactions, I feared that people would laugh at or dismiss my ideas or questions, so I stayed silent. But eventually, I dared to message one of my first mentors and now friend Brad Gustafson. I had read his work about flipping staff meetings and had a specific question about an aspect of the work he was leading. I wrote down what I wanted to say and practiced it twice before hitting the Voxer button to record my message. Then I immediately wanted to reverse time and erase it!

Thirty minutes later, I noticed that he had responded. Full transparency: I was worried about what he would say. The fear in my inner thoughts went dark. I was afraid he would think my question was silly or naïve, or that he would call my boss and tell him I had no business leading (I told you my inner voice goes dark early)! I finally hit the play button and was surprised by his response. It was detailed and encouraging, and he asked a few follow-up questions. I had never met him in person, and at the time I was sporting about 150 followers on Twitter. We continued the conversation, and I followed up with him a few weeks later after my first flipped staff meeting.

It is one thing to follow people on social media channels; it elevates it to an entirely different level when you can call them a friend, mentor, or colleague. Moving someone from a "follow" into your PLN makes your conversations real and meaningful.

In the next few weeks, we continued connecting on Twitter and Voxer and then found out we both would be at the same EdCamp. Our first meetup included a few other leaders (Bret Domstrand, Josh Lichty, and Luke Stordahl), and since that time, Brad and I regularly continue to connect in person and on social media. We have co-written blog posts, supported each other's sessions at conferences, done keynote conferences together, and endorsed each other's books. I wonder what would have happened if I hadn't sent that well-practiced Voxer message years ago? What if, instead of putting myself out there, I had stayed in my corner of the world, unconnected? Grace in vulnerability is like jumping into the deep end of the pool: you are nervous leading up to it, but glad when you are in the pool having fun with others. Brad is in my top five in many aspects of my personal and professional life, and it is only because I leaped to reach out and ask a question.

Building and cultivating these relationships take time and effort, but they are worth the work. It is one thing to follow people on social media channels; it elevates it to an entirely different level when you can call them a friend, mentor, or colleague. Moving someone from a "follow" into your PLN makes your conversations real and meaningful. The Facebook posts are stripped away for real-world conversations. I have shared embarrassing stories from work with my team, failures in my communication with others, stories about the hard work of leading at school, and my hopes and dreams for my students, staff, and family. Connecting with others means you have unlimited access to ideas and opportunities you might not have devised on your own. Utilizing tools like Twitter, Facebook, and Voxer gives you ways to ask deeper questions—ones that can't be answered in a 280-character tweet.

Find your five. Once you have them, start to cultivate those relationships. Make the time to meet up face to face, or send a message asking for help or advice. Challenge yourself to ask for help, ask for feedback, and spend more time cultivating these relationships than you do perfecting an official post on social media.

LEADFORWARDSTRATEGY
Find Your Five

Here is my favorite part of leading with grace: put your vulnerability into practice and your authenticity into action. Reach out to someone new. Give a compliment, ask a question, and build a network from which you can learn and grow in your professional and personal work.

- **Who are you reading?** Do you have a favorite author? Follow them on social media, email them a question, or stay after at one of their conference sessions to connect. Leaders are always learning. Take the chance to learn and grow, and elevate the connection from reading their work to following them online, to creating a conversation.

- **What hashtags are you following?** If you can find those who follow hashtags with similar interests as you (like #LeadForward, #HackLearning, #LeadwithGrace), you might find out you have even more in common. Once you find a hashtag you relate to, challenge yourself to post an idea, action, or question to it, and take note of the responses. You'll see many ideas you never would have thought about on your own.

- **Find a time to meet face to face.** Trust me, it is worth the gas money. Leading with grace and authenticity gives you permission to jump outside of your comfort zone and learn with leaders you have admired from afar. Driving to an EdCamp, connecting at a conference, meeting up for coffee on a Saturday, or visiting their schools deepens the connections, as well as your learning.

Responding Isn't a Race

I love accomplishing inbox zero. Cleaning up my inbox is like going through my closets and swapping out my summer clothes for fall/winter. There is a sense of completion when you can say "I am done for the day" because there is nothing in the inbox. However, completing tasks and deleting emails is different than passing things back or deflecting the work you have to do.

As a principal, I went from about sixty emails a day at the elementary level to closer to two hundred at the secondary level. Yes, there are many I can delete (or if I had the patience, unsubscribe), but some of those emails are important. That doesn't make them easy to deal with or understand! And therein lies the challenge. My morning supervision time is rarely spent in the office. Instead, I am in the halls, greeting students and checking in with staff members who might have sent one of those confusing emails. Creating a space for face-to-face time allows us to go deeper into the conversation and find a collaborative solution in real time. With that in mind, I had to figure out how to balance my face-to-face interactions with being efficient and timely in my responses to email.

What I learned is that sometimes it is okay to wait to respond. If you are not in the right frame of mind, don't have all the right information, or don't have the time to create a thoughtful response, don't. A rapid-fire response might end up being completely wrong, and whatever it is, it probably doesn't need an immediate answer. Leading with grace and utilizing the soft skill of patience allows you the wait time you need to create a thoughtful response that will reap successful results.

LEAD**FORWARD**STRATEGY
Respond On Your Time, In Your Way

While we want to be efficient in our skills as leaders, we also must practice the soft skill of waiting. Utilizing the following strategies allows you to take time to respond, and will give you the chance to wait until you are ready to engage gracefully.

- **Find face-to-face time.** Schedule out-of-office time or walk the halls during passing time. Set up a meeting rather than sending the email. Connecting physically with the person who sent you an email might clear up the question more quickly and in a more personal way.

- **Never send something in a text that would be better said in person.** While a quick response is easy, it isn't necessarily right. If the meaning of the message could get lost in text translation, consider making a call, stopping by their classroom, or finding another time to say what needs to be said in person.

- **Turn it off.** I don't have work email on my phone for a reason: I need a break. Taking email off your devices and checking your inbox only at specific times when you're at home prevents you from overthinking and overworking, and allows you to focus on projects and plans at home with your family, or for yourself. Set specific times for responding to emails, and then turn it off or close it. Having notifications beeping on your phone distracts you from the important work you're doing during the day. Create rules about your email that let others know when you are checking emails, and when you are not.

   For example, when I was on a spring break trip, my out-of-office email note read like this:

Thank you for reaching out. I will be out of the office from March 15–19 with my family. I will be checking email one time a day and responding when I return to the office on March 21. Students, I hope you are having a fantastic spring break and look forward to seeing everyone back on March 21. Mrs. Cabeen.

Try to Diffuse, Not Engage

In my third year, our school really started using social media to tell our story. It was early spring, and the big event at our school was happening: the annual chicken hatching. While we were using Facebook to video stream the eggs in the incubator, I was navigating a discussion with a parent who was frustrated with my response to her request to remove the father of her child from our directory without documentation. I probably could have had a smoother delivery in my response to her. I could have invited our HR director into the meeting to support me and offer additional options, or even contacted her later in the day or week to see if there was anything else I could do to help. But instead, I just went on with the day and took a picture of the first hatched chick (Herbert), posted it to our Facebook page, and went home for the day.

After dinner, I received a "911" text from a staff member to check Facebook. I logged in and looked at that cute picture introducing Herbert to our extended school family, and then read one of the comments: "Mrs. Cabeen takes better care of those chicks than the kids!"

After that comment came an onslaught of remarks either defending me, directing the parent to call me, or engaging in the discussion. Some of the comments were from parents (including my own—thanks Mom!), some were from community members, and even staff members jumped in. And we were only fifteen minutes into the Facebook comment conversation. Being new in this situation, I quickly figured out how to stop the comments on the post and put the parent on a brief Facebook timeout (she could see the posts but not comment on them publicly).

Leading with grace on social media means that sometimes you will leave an interaction and feel like you lost. As a leader, though, you must learn to diffuse situations rather than engage in them.

Some of you reading this will judge my response. Others would have jumped into the Facebook fight. Still others might be thinking this is why I shouldn't have used social media in the first place.

Here is the deal: during the six years I was on that campus using social media, that was the one post that caused a negative feeling in my gut and shed a negative light on our school.

Even on Twitter, I have found that some people are just waiting to catch you. A spelling error, a post that upsets them, or a quote they want to question whether I cited correctly. I have had incredible friends text or direct message me if they see something I should rethink, or ask to have a further discussion around the topic. But then others will retweet and attempt to "shame" me. How *dare* you say "their" instead of "there"? All your degrees should be taken away and you should lose your job immediately...

You will never win a fight on social media, but don't use that as an excuse to stop telling your school story. Leading with grace on social media means that sometimes you will leave an interaction and feel like you lost. As a leader, though, you must learn to diffuse situations rather than engage in them. Don't take on that difficult parent. No, backing off is not always a sign of weakness. It's a sign that you are accessing your graceful skills of integrity and reacting and responding to the post like you would to the real person.

LEAD**FORWARD**STRATEGY
Keep the Communication Positive and Moving Forward

Leading with grace might mean you have to model these skills for those who follow you. If you make a mistake, own it and fix it. If you are growing in your soft skills, you'll be able to pause, assess, and keep from making that mistake in the first place.

- **Say you are sorry.** While you can't apologize for another person's actions, you can apologize for how those actions make someone else feel. When I am cc'd on an email that is less than productive to a teacher from a parent, I call the teacher and apologize. This practice has caught some by surprise, but my intention is clear: "I am sorry if this person's words hurt or have dismissed the incredible work you do every day and I know the impact you have." After the initial apology, we work to find the best way to respond and move forward. Acknowledging the elephant in the room (or in the email) is important when it comes to maintaining relationships and checking on those you care about.

- **Don't reply, retweet, or respond in anger.** Our students, families, and staff members can be hurt by our actions, and they can intentionally or unintentionally respond in ways that hurt us back. Instead of continuing the back and forth, stop the conversation electronically and ask to meet face to face. The other person might be trying to tell you something, and taking the time to keep that conversation private and respectful lets them know that they matter and that you have time for them in person.

- **Let it go.** Too often, we harbor hurt feelings from a post or a tweet for way too long. Once the situation is resolved, delete the tweet, text, or post from your mind. True forgiveness means to accept the apology, move forward, and not bring it up down the road.

MOVINGFORWARD

Technology is changing every minute, and we can't ban devices in our schools forever. Learning how to leverage technology and push through the errors, mistakes, and misunderstandings allows us to communicate better on multiple platforms.

While I stated earlier that you will never win a fight on social media, that isn't a reason to stop using technology altogether. Don't quit. Yes, someone might make a complaint, comment, or false statement about you or your school. It isn't what they say; it is how you respond. Take the time to read through the tweet, post, or text to find the underlying meaning. And if you can't find it, pick up the phone and make a personal call. Just because a written message is faster, doesn't mean it is the right thing to do in times of conflict. Face-to-face and phone conversations still convey the soft skills, facial expressions, and emotional tones in the other person's voice better than ALL CAPITAL LETTERS EVER WILL.

Moving forward means having the vulnerability to lead on social media and using technology as a novice, not an expert. Start an Instagram account for your classroom or school and have students help you with the setup and captions. Start using #BookSnap to share your recent activities in your office for students and staff to see. Join educators at #LeadForward and #LeadwithGrace. And if the negative comments come in, use grace to respond in time and with the right tools.

CHAPTER 7
LEADFORWARDJOURNAL

Snooze, mute, or delete?

What platforms are draining my mind and taking time away from interactions face to face? Take a detox from that platform, and reflect here on how the time away impacts my emotional state.

_____

_____

_____

_____

_____

_____

_____

Find my five

Who are five people I follow and look up to on social media?

_____

_____

_____

_____

_____

_____

_____

Use this space to draft quick notes for them, or talk with them at an event and let them know the impact they have made on my life and leadership.

_____

_____

_____

_____

_____

_____

_____

_____

Unplug all cords

How am I recharging regularly?

_____

_____

_____

_____

_____

_____

Share your journal entries and ideas at #LeadForward on Twitter.

CHAPTER 9

Grace with Yourself
Pause in the Pace of All This Grace

*Of the things I'm learning to leave behind, one
of the heaviest is the opinion of others.*
— SHAUNA NIEQUIST, AUTHOR OF *PRESENT OVER PERFECT*

THIS IS THE final chapter for a reason. Grace in your day-to-day interactions with others requires a heavy dose of grace for yourself as well. Leading with integrity, walking authentically, sharing your vulnerabilities, all while building empathy, can be emotionally and physically exhausting. Giving yourself grace in this work means (gasp) you will not be perfect. Leading with grace is messy, it is hard, it can feel like an uphill battle, and then all of a sudden it will click. A student will comment, a parent will thank you, or out of the blue, another teacher will compliment you on a skill that you feel you struggle to build in every interaction. Walk into this chapter and bring your messy, mistake-making, imperfect self, and join the rest of us on this journey.

Play in the Band

Do you tell your students what you love? So often, we ask our students about their interests, dreams, and passions while neglecting to share our own. Building authentic relationships with others is a two-way street. You can't be real with them unless you reveal a little about yourself. One of the more unconventional parts of who I am is that I have been a percussionist since I was in sixth grade. I went to college as a music major and continue to play in church bands and community orchestras, all without telling my students. In essence, a part of me that has been with me the longest was missing from my students' background knowledge of who I was outside of the school, or even inside the walls.

This year all of that changed. During the long Minnesota winter, I stepped outside of my comfort zone and into the band room during the seventh hour to audition for a percussion part in the upcoming eighth grade spring band concert. At first, I was highly confident. The piece was sight-readable, I knew the rhythm, and the key signature was no problem. The challenge came when I faced the students.

The surprise on their faces said a lot. *You play drums, Mrs. Cabeen?* It was like they had just found out their principal was a person. When I started to play, their surprised looks were replaced by smiles. To these eighth-graders, I had just revealed a secret to them, and they knew it. They learned more about me and learned that the adults who support them are more than what they see from 8 a.m. to 3 p.m.

Grace and vulnerability aren't reserved just for the professional side of your life. Take the risk to share your personal passions with those you serve and those you lead, and you will give others a chance to see the bigger part of who you are, in and outside of the office.

For the next three weeks, I practiced in the percussion pit with the other drummers. Concert night arrived and I was no longer a principal, but a real member of the band. On concert day, I was peppered with questions: Would my family come? Was I nervous? Was I ready? That night, I sat with my students, as a student. I won't lie; I was nervous. Practicing with the students was one thing, but performing in front of their parents and my supervisor was another. In the end, I did it. I survived and had a chance to show my students a whole new side to me. And I was able to give myself the grace to be myself, rather than trying to be only the professional, strait-laced person I thought others expected.

Grace and vulnerability aren't reserved just for the professional side of your life. Take the risk to share your personal passions with those you serve and those you lead, and you will give others a chance to see the bigger part of who you are, in and outside of the office. You will also give yourself the chance to shine a bit more.

LEAD**FORWARD**STRATEGY
Try Out

Deep breath in and out on this one. Grace with yourself requires a little bit of transparency. Being who you are and sharing your talents with others isn't easy, but it is almost always right. The more we show up and share with others, the more likely they will do the same with us. So what is something you have wanted to do but were afraid to try?

- **Show off your talents.** Surprise your students in the band room, art room, library, theater, basketball court, or swimming pool. You should share who you are outside of the school walls, for their enrichment and your own.

- **Share the other chapters to your story.** By opening up and telling students (and staff) more about who you are, and even who you were before you became who you are now, will allow the grace of deeper importance in relationships.

- **Be scared.** So often, we ask students to stand in front of the class to speak, submit an assignment that was hard for them, or even try a new table in the lunchroom. But we haven't experienced anything like that in years. Get out of your comfort zone and be transparent by modeling that for others. Share your fears and show students how to overcome them. You'll deepen your relationships with your students and give yourself a chance to grow as well.

Get the Blinds

During the most difficult time in my personal life, I learned how quickly a situation at home could impact my ability to do my "day job." In August of 2011, an adoption I had been working toward terminated. Years of paperwork, process documentations, travels to Ethiopia … all erased in a five-minute phone call. While my therapist would call this time of loss ambiguous, I would just say the loss was big and devastating. Two weeks later, school was going to start, and I started to stuff down my personal emotions and feelings in an attempt to focus on the work I was starting up again. As the assistant principal of a middle school, I'd found that I needed to keep my own emotions in check if I was going to navigate the hormones of sixth- through eighth-graders, as well as the family members and staff connected to these young people.

For a while, I was able to "survive" the season, but then it started to happen. Out of nowhere, I would start crying. I could never pick the trigger because there were so many. A toddler about the size of our son walking into school to get his older sibling, a student asking when we were going to Africa to get our child, or even a thoughtful word or check-in from a staff member. Whatever it was, the waterworks started.

I tried visualizing Tom Hanks from *A League of Their Own* yelling at me, "There is no crying in principaling!" I started to establish walls to protect the vulnerable side of myself from the world. My interactions became less authentic, and the sadness on the inside became apparent on the outside. The leadership team at our middle school was incredibly supportive. While I felt guilty for my emotional outbursts, they were working behind the scenes to make sure I had a support team to walk alongside me in this difficult pit.

One piece to this story is that my front-facing office wall was all windows. This made it difficult to find a safe space to have a meltdown. I had spent weeks hiding out in a bathroom in the dean's office when the principal's administrative assistant came into my office with a tape measure and fabric. Within weeks, I had blinds. Initially, I was embarrassed and felt guilty that the team had to support my emotional stability during this time of my life. But leading with grace and vulnerability means that sometimes we need to ask for help and support through the dark challenges and seasons of our personal lives. As leaders, recognizing that we can't always keep clear boundaries between work and home, and modeling ways to seek support and resources, are essential in growing this type of culture for our schools. When the leader loses something as precious as a child, it is okay to let others know. Allow them to help you through the grief to the other side of the journey. Giving yourself the space to be sad and accepting help from others helps you to grow both as an individual and as a leader.

LEADFORWARDSTRATEGY
See Something, Feel Something, Say Something

Leading with grace means recognizing that sometimes you need to seek support outside of yourself, and as difficult as it may be, ask for help from others during certain seasons.

- **Ask for help.** It could be blinds for a window or asking to leave work a little early on a particularly tough day. Reaching out and asking for help isn't a weakness; it takes strength and courage to admit. Start practicing this in your day-to-day life. When you're having a tough day, look for small ways that others can help. If your season is particularly dark, look for larger resources to help you.

- **Recognize the signs.** Start to look for signs that you're heading into a season of darkness. Finding triggers, such as dates on the calendar, allows you to prepare mentally and emotionally for what might come. Knowing ahead of time that a dark season is coming will make it easier for you to grant grace for yourself in asking for and accepting help.

- **Listen to your people.** It wasn't easy, but my friend and mentor Ron stuck by me through that entire season. He sat with me after school was over, and encouraged me to seek professional help when he knew I needed it. Find your person and listen to them. Have the grace for yourself that you would have for others, and allow yourself to lean on someone and hear them when they give you advice.

Using Dark Seasons for Growth

The analogies of seasons are used across literary genres. Seasons mark changes in our years, and at times, changes in our lives. Each one of us goes through storms that are brief and storms that last for extended periods. Regardless of the duration of the storm, finding ways to ask for help and seek care for yourself is essential to walking through the storm with the confidence necessary to survive.

For me, during the storm of our adoption, I lost a sense of joy in things I previously enjoyed. Waking up became more difficult, engaging with friends became more of a chore, and I found myself constantly under clouds of sadness. At this time, I noticed those around me struggling to find the right words to say, and honestly, I don't think anyone could have said anything to heal my heart. Some of my dearest friends started to send cards—sometimes funny ones, and at other times, more serious ones. Another friend would drop a coffee off just at the right time, and my book club sent a beautiful bouquet of flowers. Another of my dearest friends offered to clean my toilets. Yes, reread that sentence. This incredible person was willing to do absolutely anything to help me during my sadness.

Readers, when you find that person in your life, don't let them go. This group of people cared enough to check-in, call, or send texts at the exact moment I needed them. As the season started to stabilize, I found a small joy in running again, I forced myself back out into social circles, and I slowly reintegrated back into adoption circles and started to move forward in our new normal. And I now had a better understanding of myself and those around me.

Coming out on the other side, I found that I was grateful for the experience, as it helped me build strength in asking for help. Vulnerability only grows and enhances your ability to lead when you use it. While storms are not the most enjoyable seasons, I am learning to appreciate the rain and the growing that occurs as I go through them.

LEADFORWARDSTRATEGY
Finding Ways to Thrive in Difficult Seasons

Walking through any season can't be a passive experience. Take an active role in recognizing your needs and seeking help, and you will better maintain your support networks as you learn and grow.

- **Seek support.** When you are in a season, reach out for help. Talk with a pastor, find a therapist, or seek assistance from your medical provider. Don't wait for the "right time" to ask. That's not fair to yourself, and it's not fair to those who are depending on you. The time is now.

- **Find that friend**. Earlier, I spoke about not having to be the one who brings the hot dish or casserole to someone in a season of struggle. I further spoke about being the person who can listen instead. Who is in your circle, and for what can you lean on them? Which one of your friends knows exactly what you need, when you need it? Every one of us deserves a friend who knows what we need in our dark times—even if it is unconventional.

- **Buy a box.** Seriously. Go out and buy a box to store all the notes you get from those who believe in you and your work. Print out those emails that bring tears to your eyes. Save the artwork and apologies from students. Store them in a box in your office and bring them back to the surface when you are struggling in a dark season. It is essential that we remind ourselves that our team cares for and celebrates us.

Stop Worrying, Start Focusing

Has this happened to you? You have a project, a dream, or an idea that you can't get started. You set time on the calendar, find a space to work, and then get distracted by all the reasons not to start. I am the self-appointed queen of procrastinating on purpose. I mean, I should look at the new line of Away travel bags for an hour before working on an upcoming keynote. Or I should spend my Friday night in front of the TV instead of the computer screen, working on this section of the book. Too often, I let the static of what society tells me to do drown out the work that needs to get done. Honestly, if I just did what I was supposed to do, I would have time at the end to binge-watch a few episodes of my favorite Netflix show guilt-free.

One of my biggest time sucks is creating graphics. I was an elementary teacher who could never get her bulletin boards quite right. Today, I am the one who will spend hours on the colors and fonts for a graphic for the newsletter or a post on Instagram. Taking a step back, I can see that the graphic that took two minutes looks just as good as the one that took twenty minutes, and in the end, what matters is the amount of time I have left to complete other tasks. Starting a blog was equally hard. It took weeks to get the right layout, tabs, and titles. I fretted over the cover picture and the titles for each section. I played around with having the Twitter feed on the right side or the bottom.

I am almost embarrassed to admit how long it took me to even settle on the title: principalinbalance.wordpress.com. If I could do it all over again, I would have set a timer on my phone and had key deliverables done within a timeframe. I would have put each task on a separate sticky note and thrown them away after each task was done, and if I wanted to go back and tweak something, I would have had to go back and grab that note out of the garbage. No thank you.

Recently, I found myself in a full panic attack. I was having a hard time breathing and focusing, and became more emotional than normal. When I slowed down my brain to figure out what was wrong, I was almost embarrassed. I was panicking because I hadn't finished packing for a family trip, happening in three days! Recalibrating and not allowing ourselves to become consumed with tasks, and instead focusing on being calm and content in every moment, will help us put priorities back in focus.

Grace with yourself is a free pass to just start something. Stop worrying about what others will say, whether anyone will read that blog post, or if your essay for the written part of the upcoming interview is any good. The only way you are going to get better and lead with authenticity is to start doing something in creative and unconventional ways. If you write from the heart and make sure your best self shows up in your words and actions, you have completed a job well. And for goodness' sake, just pick your favorite font and don't spend more than five minutes on it!

LEAD**FORWARD**STRATEGY
Rip It Off Like a Band-Aid

What is something you have wanted to do but were afraid to start? Leading with authenticity means you are fueled by a passion and a calling. Having grace for yourself means you give yourself the go-ahead to try those things. Don't hide it; start doing it!

- **Set a timer.** Write a letter of recommendation or finish an evaluation or report, and give yourself a set amount of time to keep you from questioning yourself. Set a timer, and when it goes off, be done with that project and move on to the next one.

- **Make a goal.** Do you want to start blogging, or create a new unit in your class? Write down the goal and set markers for success. Writing it down will make it more real, and those markers will help you brainstorm and build out your plan.

- **Not everything needs a response.** Just because someone sends you a text about an idea they have on Saturday night, doesn't mean you need to respond to them. Setting boundaries and office hours on your personal time and devices are essential to maintaining healthy relationships and your sanity! Someone might send, share, or say something to you, but that doesn't mean it (or they) requires an immediate response or even a response at all. Have the grace to give yourself room to breathe and think before you respond. Set it as one of your boundaries, and stick to it!

- **Tell others.** I use the hashtag #principalinbalance to tell others about new projects, marathons, and other ideas I have brewing. That accountability is essential to me. If I've put something out into the world as an intention, I'm more likely to start and finish it.

Find a Fight Song

This work can be daunting. There will be days that you might need an extra dose of courage to walk through the doors. As a former music therapist, I know the therapeutic benefits that music can play in many aspects of life and work. Music can help identify feelings, relieve stress, and build confidence in the work to come. Think about your favorite song; what happens when you listen to it? What memories come to mind when you hear it? Finding out and archiving these experiences will help you build the self-confidence you need to continue to persevere in this work of leading in school and life.

If you were to look at my phone, you would see multiple playlists with various reasons to listen. Running 2019 has a list of songs to help me prepare for an upcoming marathon. Workout Wednesday includes songs to blast in the halls of the middle school when we need a little smile during our active supervision. Balance 2016 is an archived playlist of songs that help me recalibrate, focus, and attend to the work ahead. Dream Big, well, that is my confidence-boosting playlist. The one I need when a big decision lies ahead.

Create a playlist of songs that make you smile, prepare you for the day, and give you the confidence you need to make the decisions that need to happen. Create several playlists for different feels and needs, but make sure they all pick you up in some way. What is your musical mantra? What song always pumped you up in your twenties? What songs make you feel unbeatable, and what songs allow you to cry when you need it? Figure out which songs belong where, and then build your playlists of fight songs. Finding the musical inspiration to trudge through the muck of leading with grace just might be the push you need.

LEAD**FORWARD**STRATEGY
Tune In to Courage

- **Make a playlist.** What kind of playlists do you need? To start with, put together one for pumping yourself up and one for allowing yourself to relax. Then start to refine them. What music works best for working out? What music suits you when you're driving to a big meeting? What music just makes you feel good? Put playlists together for all of them, and label them appropriately.

- **Keep them handy.** Next up, make sure your playlists are well organized and always available. Use an app on your phone to collect and label them, and make sure you know how to easily hook up your phone to your stereo. This will keep those theme songs handy when you need them.

- **Dance it up.** Seriously, research shows dancing can reduce anxiety and depression, and boost self-esteem. Turn on the music, stand up, and shake it off.

Leading with grace means allowing yourself to receive it, not just giving it freely to everyone around you.

MOVING**FORWARD**

Running into resistance is a good sign that you are doing what you need to do.

— DR. HENRY CLOUD AND DR. JOHN TOWNSEND,
CO-AUTHORS OF *BOUNDARIES*

I've wondered why there weren't many books out on soft skills and graceful leadership. That was ... until I started writing this book myself. Leading with grace is like fighting an uphill battle. Navigating all the moving parts is difficult, especially when they aren't parts at all, but rather people. When I focused in on this work, I felt like I was either on top of the highest mountain as a peak performer or in a deep pit that felt like quicksand. These polar opposite feelings took a physical and emotional toll on me. As I continue in this work and lead with a lens of grace, the mountains and pits have been replaced with rolling hills and valleys, neither of which I stay in for long. I no longer look at the end of the day and feel overwhelmed by what is left, but instead feel overjoyed by what I have done. Leading with grace means allowing yourself to receive it, not just giving it freely to everyone around you.

This work is ongoing and can be exhausting, but the lessons learned will help you grow even more. Leading forward in this work means you will continue to run up the hills and down into the valleys, but that shows you that what you're doing is working. What season are you in, or did you just come out of? Reflect on what you've learned, where you can get better, and where you can help yourself and others as you continue on this path of leading with grace.

CHAPTER 9
LEAD**FORWARD**JOURNAL

Pause button

How am I finding pause in the pace of leading with grace?

_____

_____

_____

Mindfulness

Find a mindfulness app, put my phone down, go for a walk, or take a few deep breaths. Whatever I choose to do, commit to engaging in five minutes of mindfulness for the next ten days. Write down how I will accomplish this.

_____

_____

_____

Journal

Purchase a journal for my daily thoughts, affirmations, and gratitude. End each journal with the following prompts:

I am grateful for:	I am looking forward to:

Share your journal entries and ideas at #LeadForward on Twitter.

Instead of Moving On, Move Forward

THANK YOU. I am grateful for you. For recognizing that grace is accessible to all of us, and in today's world, it is necessary.

It is time to bring back difficult conversations without harboring hurtful feelings. We are ready to make big changes in how we lead, based on how we communicate. It is time to think more about others than what others might think about us. Having hard conversations doesn't feel nice, but they are necessary to move our relationships and organizations forward.

Throughout this book, I have shared my failures in this work—small, big, and really big. Leading with grace takes those key skills—authenticity, vulnerability, empathy, and integrity—and embeds them into who you are, not who you think you need to be. While working with soft skills is messy, if you can do it as your best self, it will be worth the work. While I started this book sharing my *Frogger* career story, one thing I have learned is that you must lead your life like you are leaving your legacy. We never know what tomorrow will bring: a new job, new students, new dreams. If you lead every day with the best effort to model these soft skills in your way, you can be sure that people will remember you for what you did and how you did it.

Here is my final piece of advice: don't let the fear of perfection stop you from starting. Humans are unpredictable. So if you are walking into this work thinking you will hit 100 percent every time, I hate to tell you this, but you will be wrong. Learning to lead with grace means being willing to recognize that you will *not* hit the mark every time. Being humble, asking for help, and seeking forgiveness when things go wrong are essential skills when it comes to leading with grace and building stronger relationships with everyone you interact with.

So instead of moving on from circumstances and situations, move forward. Don't look away from what happened, because you will miss out on the lessons you learned. Move forward with the knowledge of every interaction, every circumstance, and every relationship you have built. Use that knowledge to continue to grow in grace throughout your life and work.

About the Author

Photo by Eric Johnson

JESSICA CABEEN IS the principal of Ellis Middle School in Austin, Minnesota. Before that, she was the principal of the "Happiest Place in Southeastern Minnesota," the Woodson Kindergarten Center. She has been an assistant middle school principal, a special education assistant director, and special education teacher.

Jessica received her bachelor's degree in music therapy at the University of Wisconsin-Eau Claire. She attended the University of St. Thomas for her master's degree in special education. Jessica has administrative licenses from Hamline University in both the principalship and director of special education. She continues her learning as a facilitator of the Minnesota Principal Academy and was a facilitator of the Minnesota PreK–3 Principal Academy, a partnership with the Minnesota Department of Education and the Minnesota Elementary Principal Association.

She started her career as a music therapist in Illinois and Iowa. She moved into the school setting as a music therapist for the Saint Paul Public Schools in Saint Paul, Minnesota, and then became an autism teacher for the district and an administrative intern with district Special Education Administration. She moved to Austin, Minnesota, as a special education supervisor and then an assistant principal at Ellis Middle School. She is passionate about learning and leading, and enjoys the challenge of building relationships with all ages—but mainly kindergarten and seventh- and eighth-graders.

Jessica was awarded the NAESP/VINCI Digital Leader of Early Learning Award in 2016, and in 2017 was named the Minnesota National Distinguished Principal. Jessica is the author of *Hacking Early Learning* and co-authored *Balance Like a Pirate*. She is a sought-after speaker and trainer and enjoys getting to learn and lead with other educators across the nation. But at the end of the day, her boys are the real loves of her life. She is married to Rob and their sons are Kenny and Isaiah. Oh, and she is Mom to Rigby, the family dog.

She enjoys connecting and growing her Professional Learning Community. Please reach out to her via Twitter and Instagram @JessicaCabeen and on her website at www.jessicacabeen.com

More from the
LEAD**FORWARD**SERIES

LEADFORWARD

Stories & Strategies for Teacher Leaders

The Lead Forward Series from Times 10 Publications features world-class teacher leaders sharing the stories and strategies that will inspire you to be the best you can be, while always leading forward. Learn more about the series and our team at WeLeadForward.com.

Sanée Bell

Intentional Strategies
for Impactful Leadership

LEADFORWARD

BE EXCELLENT ON PURPOSE

Intentional Strategies for Impactful Leadership

By Sanée Bell (@saneebell)

"**Be Excellent on Purpose.**" I don't know many people who wake up each day and say, "I want to be average, below average, or completely ineffective today." Most people intend to have the kind of day that allows them to feel good about their accomplishments and contributions. That doesn't mean everyone understands what it means to be *excellent*.

So what exactly does it take to be excellent? And how do you do it on purpose? To *Be Excellent on Purpose* means following a clear-cut path: being intentional with your time, the company you keep, and where you focus your thinking and energy. Do those things and you're taking the steps you need to take toward being intentional about being *excellent*.

In this inaugural book in the Lead Forward Series, longtime teacher, author, presenter, and Principal of the Year Sanée Bell shares personal and professional stories and strategies that will make your leadership intentional and impactful. She shows how to become a leader who can maintain motivation despite the challenges, how teachers can motivate students who are apathetic about learning, and how leaders can turn around underperforming schools. Get ready to break the mold and lead forward with excellence!

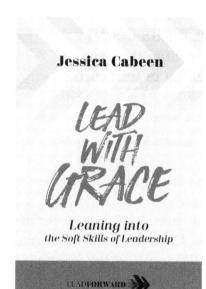

Jessica Cabeen

LEAD WITH GRACE

Leaning into
the Soft Skills of Leadership

LEADFORWARD

LEAD WITH GRACE
Leaning Into the Soft Skills of Leadership

By Jessica Cabeen (@jessicacabeen)

With technology, we interact with families, students, and staff 24/7, not just during the school day or working hours. Pressures and demands at work can sway who we are and how we do it into a personality that favors more online likes than the authentic interactions we need to establish deep relationships with the students we serve. **So, we need grace more than ever.**

Throughout this book, you'll read stories and strategies that will allow you to walk away with key practices and exercises that will build confidence so you can extend grace with others. School leader, author, and keynote speaker Jessica Cabeen provides frames that will empower anyone—teacher, principal, parent, or superintendent—to lead with grace.

Chrissy Romano

Unleashing
the True Potential of Introverts

QUIET KIDS COUNT
Unleashing the True Potential of Introverts

By Chrissy Romano Arrabito (@TheConnectedEDU)

The grade level or content you teach doesn't matter; you will have them sitting in your room—the introverts, the quiet kids, and the not-so-quiet, but introverts just the same. They don't cause trouble and, for the most part, they earn good grades. But these are the kids who tend to fade into the background and slip through the cracks. The ones who are so often overlooked, or in some cases, misunderstood.

In Lead Forward Series book number two, Chrissy Romano Arrabito provides **a guidebook to help you better understand the nature of *all* types of introverts** and to allay the misconceptions about them. She provides useful tips and strategies to help these students reach their full potential. *Quiet Kids Count* is a call to action for educators to step up and meet the needs of ALL learners—not just the ones who command the most attention in our schools.

Suzy Brooks
Matthew X. Joseph

MODERN
MENTOR

Reimagining
Teacher Mentorship

LEADFORWARD ➤➤

MODERN MENTOR
Reimagining Teacher Mentorship

By Suzy Brooks (@simplysuzy)
& Matthew X. Joseph
(@matthewxjoseph)

As modern mentors, how can we shift our practices as individuals or make widespread change happen in our systems? Mentoring is not the process of checking a box; it is the process of developing colleagues who eventually work alongside us in a challenging profession where collaboration, connection, and consistency are all vital for our students.

If you want to know exactly what you will get, you need a menu of strategies! **This book showcases ways to develop mentoring programs,** designed to assist teachers in becoming strong mentors and to assist new teachers in getting the most out of their mentoring relationship.

Veteran educators, recognized school leaders, and expert mentors Suzy Brooks and Matthew X. Joseph bring you the Stories and Strategies that will help you turn novice educators into EduStars.

MORE FROM
TIMES 10 BOOKS

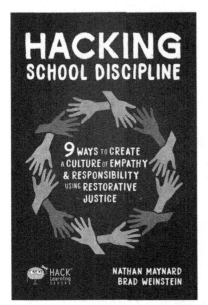

HACKING SCHOOL DISCIPLINE

9 Ways to Create a Culture of Empathy & Responsibility Using Restorative Justice

By Nathan Maynard (@nmaynardedu) and Brad Weinstein (@weinsteinedu)

Are you or your teachers frustrated with carrots and sticks, detention rooms, and suspension—antiquated school discipline practices that simply do not work with the students entering our classrooms today? Our kids have complex needs, and we must empower and embrace them with restorative practices that not only change behaviors but transform students into productive citizens, accountable for their own actions. In a book that should become your new blueprint for school discipline, teachers, presenters, and school leaders Nathan Maynard and Brad Weinstein demonstrate how to eliminate punishment and build a culture of responsible students and independent learners. **Before you suspend another student**... read *Hacking School Discipline*, and build a school environment that promotes responsible learners who never need to be punished. Then watch learning soar, teachers smile, and your entire community rejoice.

HACKING EDUCATION
10 Quick Fixes For Every School

By Mark Barnes (@markbarnes19) & Jennifer Gonzalez (@cultofpedagogy)

In the award-winning first Hack Learning Series book, *Hacking Education*, Mark Barnes and Jennifer Gonzalez employ decades of teaching experience and hundreds of discussions with education thought leaders to show you how to find and hone the quick fixes that every school and classroom need. Using a Hacker's mentality, they provide **one Aha moment after another** with 10 Quick Fixes For Every School—solutions to everyday problems and teaching methods that any teacher or administrator can implement immediately.

"Barnes and Gonzalez don't just solve problems; they turn teachers into hackers—a transformation that is right on time."

—Don Wettrick, Author of *Pure Genius*

HACKING PROJECT BASED LEARNING
10 Easy Steps to PBL and Inquiry in the Classroom

By Ross Cooper (@rosscoops31) and Erin Murphy (@murphysmusings5)

As questions and mysteries around PBL and inquiry continue to swirl, experienced classroom teachers and school administrators Ross Cooper and Erin Murphy have written a book that will empower those intimidated by PBL to cry, "I can do this!" while at the same time providing added value for those who are already familiar with the process. Impacting teachers and leaders around the world, *Hacking Project Based Learning* demystifies what PBL is all about with **10 hacks that construct a simple path** that educators and students can easily follow to achieve success. Forget your prior struggles with project based learning. This book makes PBL an amazing gift you can give all students tomorrow!

"*Hacking Project Based Learning* is a classroom essential. Its ten simple 'hacks' will guide you through the process of setting up a learning environment in which students will thrive from start to finish."

—DANIEL H. PINK, *NEW YORK TIMES* BESTSELLING AUTHOR OF *DRIVE*

HACKING ASSESSMENT
10 Ways To Go Gradeless In a Traditional Grades School
By Starr Sackstein (@mssackstein)

In the bestselling *Hacking Assessment,* award-winning teacher and world-renowned formative assessment expert Starr Sackstein unravels one of education's oldest mysteries: how to assess learning without grades—even in a school that uses numbers, letters, GPAs, and report cards. While many educators can only muse about the possibility of a world without grades, teachers like Sackstein are **reimagining education**. In this unique, eagerly-anticipated book, Sackstein shows you exactly how to create a remarkable no-grades classroom like hers, a vibrant place where students grow, share, thrive, and become independent learners who never ask, "What's this worth?"

"The beauty of the book is that it is not an empty argument against grades—but rather filled with valuable alternatives that are practical and will help to refocus the classroom on what matters most."

—Adam Bellow, White House Presidential Innovation Fellow

HACKING LEADERSHIP
10 Ways Great Leaders Inspire Learning That Teachers, Students, and Parents Love

By Joe Sanfelippo (@joe_sanfelippo) and Tony Sinanis (@tonysinanis)

In the runaway bestseller *Hacking Leadership*, internationally known school leaders Joe Sanfelippo and Tony Sinanis bring readers inside schools that few stakeholders have ever seen—places where students not only come first but have a unique voice in teaching and learning. Sanfelippo and Sinanis ignore the bureaucracy that stifles many leaders, focusing instead on building a culture of **engagement, transparency and, most importantly, fun**. *Hacking Leadership* has superintendents, principals, and teacher leaders around the world employing strategies they never before believed possible and learning how to lead from the middle. Want to revolutionize teaching and learning at your school or district? *Hacking Leadership* is your blueprint. Read it today, energize teachers and learners tomorrow!

"The authors do a beautiful job of helping leaders focus inward, instead of outward. This is an essential read for leaders who are, or want to lead, learner-centered schools."

—GEORGE COUROS, AUTHOR OF *THE INNOVATOR'S MINDSET*

HACKING SCHOOL CULTURE
Designing Compassionate Classrooms

By Angela Stockman (@angelastockman) and Ellen Feig Gray (@ellenfeiggray)

Bullying prevention and character-building programs are deepening our awareness of how today's kids struggle and how we might help, but many agree: they aren't enough to create school cultures where students and staff flourish. This inspired Angela Stockman and Ellen Feig Gray to begin seeking out systems and educators who were getting things right. Their experiences taught them that the real game changers are using a human-centered approach. Inspired by other design thinkers, many teachers are creating learning environments where seeking a greater understanding of themselves and others is the highest standard. They're also realizing that **compassion is best cultivated in the classroom,** not the boardroom or the auditorium. It's here that we learn how to pull one another close. It's here that we begin to negotiate the distances between us, too.

"Hacking School Culture: Designing Compassionate Classrooms is a valuable addition to the Hack Learning Series. It provides concrete support and suggestions for teachers to improve their interactions with their students at the same time they enrich their own professional experiences. Although primarily aimed at K–12 classrooms, the authors' insightful suggestions have given me, a veteran college professor, new insights into positive classroom dynamics which I have already begun to incorporate into my classes."

—LOUISE HAINLINE, PH.D., PROFESSOR OF PSYCHOLOGY, BROOKLYN COLLEGE OF CUNY

HACKING EARLY LEARNING
10 Building Blocks to Success in Pre-K–3 That All Teachers and School Leaders Should Know

By Jessica Cabeen (@jessicacabeen)

School readiness, closing achievement gaps, partnering with families, and innovative learning are just a few of the reasons the **early learning years are the most critical** years in a child's life. In what ways have schools lost the critical components of early learning—preschool through third grade—and how can we intentionally bring those ideas and instructional strategies back? In *Hacking Early Learning*, kindergarten school leader, early childhood education specialist, and Minnesota State Principal of the Year Jessica Cabeen provides strategies for teachers, principals, and district administrators for best practices in preschool through third grade, including connecting these strategies to all grade levels.

"Jessica Cabeen is not afraid to say she's learned from her mistakes and misconceptions. But it is those mistakes and misconceptions that qualify her to write this book, with its wonderfully user-friendly format. For each problem specified, there is a hack and actionable advice presented as "What You Can Do Tomorrow" and "A Blueprint for Full Implementation." Jessica's leadership is informed by both head and heart and, because of that, her wisdom will be of value to those who wish to teach and lead in the early childhood field."

—Rae Pica, Early Childhood Education Keynote Speaker and Author of *What If Everybody Understood Child Development?*

Adam Chamberlin & Svetoslav Matejic

QUIT POINT:

Understanding Apathy, Engagement, and Motivation in the Classroom

By Adam Chamberlin and Svetoslav Matejic (@pomme_ed)

Two classroom teachers grew tired of apathy in their classrooms, so they asked two simple but crucial questions: Why do students quit? And more importantly, what should we do about it? In *Quit Point: Understanding Apathy, Engagement, and Motivation in the Classroom*, authors Chamberlin and Matejic present a new way of approaching those issues. The Quit Point—their theory on how, why, and when people quit and how to stop quitting before it happens—will **transform how teachers reach the potential of each and every student.**

Quit Point reveals how to confront apathy and build student engagement; interventions to challenge students to keep going; and how to experience a happier, more fulfilling, teaching experience—starting tomorrow. Researchers, school leaders, and teachers have wondered for centuries what makes students stop working. Now, the answer is finally here. Read *Quit Point* today and stop quitting in your school or class before it begins.

HACKING ENGAGEMENT
50 Tips & Tools to Engage Teachers and Learners Daily

By James Alan Sturtevant (@jamessturtevant)

Some students hate your class. Others are just bored. Many are too nice, or too afraid, to say anything about it. Don't let it bother you; it happens to the best of us. But now, it's **time to engage!** In *Hacking Engagement*, the seventh book in the Hack Learning Series, veteran high school teacher, author, and popular podcaster James Sturtevant provides 50—that's right five-oh—tips and tools that will engage even the most reluctant learners daily. Sold in dozens of countries around the world, *Hacking Engagement* has become an educator's go-to guide for better student engagement in all grades and subjects. In fact, this book is so popular, Sturtevant penned a follow-up, *Hacking Engagement Again*, which brings 50 more powerful strategies. Find both at HackLearningBooks.com.

HACKING DIGITAL LEARNING STRATEGIES
10 Ways to Launch EdTech Missions in Your Classroom
By Shelly Sanchez Terrell (@shellterrell)

In this breakthrough book, international EdTech presenter and NAPW Woman of the Year Shelly Sanchez Terrell demonstrates the power of EdTech Missions—lessons and projects that inspire learners to use web tools and social media to innovate, research, collaborate, problem-solve, campaign, crowd fund, crowdsource, and publish. The 10 Missions in *Hacking DLS* are more than enough to transform how teachers integrate technology, but there's also much more here. Included in the book is a **38-page Mission Toolkit**, complete with reproducible mission cards, badges, polls, and other handouts that you can copy and distribute to students immediately.

"The secret to Shelly's success as an education collaborator on a global scale is that she shares information most revered by all educators, information that is original, relevant, and vetted, combining technology with proven education methodology in the classroom. This book provides relevance to a 21st-century educator."

—THOMAS WHITBY, AUTHOR, PODCASTER, BLOGGER, CONSULTANT, CO-FOUNDER OF #EDCHAT

HACKING CLASSROOM MANAGEMENT
10 Ideas To Help You Become the Type of Teacher They Make Movies About
By Mike Roberts (@baldroberts)

Utah English Teacher of the Year and sought-after speaker Mike Roberts brings you 10 quick and easy classroom management hacks that will **make your classroom the place to be** for all your students. He shows you how to create an amazing learning environment that actually makes discipline, rules, and consequences obsolete, no matter if you're a new teacher or a 30-year veteran teacher.

"Mike writes from experience; he's learned, sometimes the hard way, what works and what doesn't, and he shares those lessons in this fine little book. The book is loaded with specific, easy-to-apply suggestions that will help any teacher create and maintain a classroom where students treat one another with respect, and where they learn."

—CHRIS CROWE, ENGLISH PROFESSOR AT BYU, PAST PRESIDENT OF ALAN, AUTHOR OF *DEATH COMING UP THE HILL, GETTING AWAY WITH MURDER: THE TRUE STORY OF THE EMMETT TILL CASE; MISSISSIPPI TRIAL, 1955*

HACKING THE WRITING WORKSHOP
Redesign with Making in Mind
By Angela Stockman (@angelastockman)

Agility matters. This is what Angela Stockman learned when she left the classroom over a decade ago to begin supporting young writers and their teachers in schools. What she learned transformed her practice and led to the publication of her primer on this topic: *Make Writing: 5 Teaching Strategies that Turn Writer's Workshop Into a Maker Space.* Now, Angela is back with more stories from the road and **plenty of new thinking to share.** In *Make Writing,* Stockman upended the traditional writing workshop by combining it with the popular ideas that drive the maker space. Now, she is expanding her concepts and strategies and breaking new ground in *Hacking the Writing Workshop.*

"Good writing is good thinking. This is a book about how to think better, for yourself and with others."

—DAVE GRAY, FOUNDER OF XPLANE, AND AUTHOR OF *THE CONNECTED COMPANY, GAMESTORMING,* AND *LIMINAL THINKING*

RESOURCES FROM TIMES 10

SITES:

times10books.com
hacklearning.org
hacklearningbooks.com
weleadforward.com
hackingquestions.com

PODCASTS:

hacklearningpodcast.com
jamesalansturtevant.com/podcast

FREE TOOLS FOR EDUCATORS:

hacklearningtoolkit.com
leadforwardpreview.com
greatleadershipwebinar.com

ON TWITTER:

@HackMyLearning
@LeadForward2
#LeadForward
#HackLearning
#ChasingGreatness
#HackingLeadership
#HackingMath
#HackingEngagement
#HackingPBL

#MakeWriting
#EdTechMissions
#HackingEarlyLearning
#CompassionateClassrooms
#HackYourLibrary
#QuitPoint
#HackingQs
#HackingSchoolDiscipline
#LeadWithGrace

HACK LEARNING ON FACEBOOK:

facebook.com/hacklearningseries
facebook.com/groups/weleadforward

HACK LEARNING ON INSTAGRAM:

hackmylearning

X10

Vision, Experience, Action

TIMES 10 is helping all education stakeholders improve every aspect of teaching and learning. We are committed to solving big problems with simple ideas. We bring you content from experts, shared through multiple channels, including books, podcasts, and an array of social networks. Our mantra is simple: Read it today; fix it tomorrow. Stay in touch with us at Times10Books.com, at #HackLearning on Twitter, and on the Hack Learning Facebook page.